Trauma-Informed Social-Emotional Toolbox
For Children & Adolescents

116 Worksheets & Skill-Building Exercises to
Support Safety, Connection & Empowerment

Lisa Weed Phifer, DEd, NCSP
Laura K. Sibbald, MA, CCC-SLP

Published by
PESI Publishing & Media
PESI, Inc.
3839 White Ave
Eau Claire, WI 54703

Cover: Amy Rubenzer
Editing: Jenessa Jackson, PhD
Layout: Amy Rubenzer & Bookmasters

ISBN: 9781683732860
Printed in the United States of America

PESI
Publishing
& Media

pesipublishing.com

About the Authors

Lisa Weed Phifer, D.Ed., NCSP, is a nationally certified school psychologist and author who has a well-established career providing school-based mental health services to children and adolescents. Phifer's work has focused on integrating cognitive-based therapy into the school setting and facilitating trauma-informed education practices. She is the lead author for *CBT Toolbox for Children & Adolescents* and the *Parenting Toolbox*. Her work has been published internationally and she has also contributed to other books and articles relating to trauma-informed practices. Dr. Phifer's most rewarding role is at home with her family, husband Jeffrey, daughter Genevieve, and goldendoodle Midas.

Laura K. Sibbald, M.A., CCC-SLP, is a nationally certified speech-language pathologist who has extensive experience supporting the social-emotional and pragmatic language needs of students and families within the Washington, D.C. metropolitan region. Laura graduated from The George Washington University in 2011 with a Master's in Speech-Language Pathology. In order to further support student growth and achievement, Laura earned additional certifications in Relationship Development Intervention (RDI), and Educational Leadership and Supervision. Laura co-authored the *Parenting Toolbox* and has developed and implemented a variety of professional learning opportunities at the local, state, and national level.

Table of Contents

Introduction 1

Chapter 1: Recognizing Trauma and Moving Forward 7

   Recognizing Trauma 7

      Social-Emotional Checklist 8

      Social-Emotional Shield 10

      Helpful or Harmful Stress 11

      Stress and the Brain 12

      Life Stressors and Control 13

      Recognizing Trauma and Adversity 14

      Short-Term vs. Ongoing Stress 15

   Creating Conversation 17

      Calm Words Cloud 18

      Word Storm 19

      Memories and Feelings 20

      Part 1: Then and Now Icons 21

      Then and Now Timeline 23

      Part 2: Now and Beyond Icons 24

      Now and Beyond Timeline 25

      What Happened? 26

      What is Bothering Me? 28

      In My Own Words 29

   Moving Forward 31

      Fight, Flight, or Freeze Feelings 32

      My Iceberg of Feelings 34

      Child Readiness Check-In 36

      Caregiver Readiness Check-In 37

      Social-Emotional Skills Inventory (Caregiver) 38

      Social-Emotional Skills Inventory (Client) 39

Chapter 2: Creating a Foundation of Safety 41

Protective Assets and Risk Factors 41

Building Protective Factors 42

Protective Bubbles 43

What Are Risks? 44

Examining Risks 45

Weighing Assets and Risks 46

Identifying Triggers 47

Threat, Thought, or Challenge? 48

Worry Workshop 50

What Triggers Your Fear Response? 52

Emotional Triggers or Reminders 53

Recognizing Triggers, Emotions, and Reactions 55

Establishing Safety 56

Safety Pyramid 57

Setting a Foundation 58

Safe Places, Safe Plans 59

Safety Gauge 60

Safe Feelings 61

Comfortable Feelings, Comfortable Me 62

Chapter 3: Building Trust and Understanding 63

Building Trust 63

Baseline Trust Profile 64

Levels of Trust 65

Leveling Up on Trust 67

Building Back Trust 68

Making Mistakes 69

Creating a Judgment-Free Contract 70

Learning to Be Open 72

Learning to Be Vulnerable 73

Empowered to Be Vulnerable 74

How Do I Perceive Others? 75

How Do I Want to Be Perceived? 76

Empathy and Humility 78

Being Humble 79

Master, Apprentice, and Intern 81

Humble at Home 82

Humble at School 84

Humble: An Empowering Reflection 86

Chapter 4: From Reliving to Relieving: Self-Regulation Strategies 89

Regulating Emotions 89

Emotions Palette 90

How Do You Feel? 91

Body Language 92

Managing Big Emotions 93

Face Your Fear 94

Feelings Addition: Add It Up 96

Coping Skills and Supports 97

Exploring Coping Skills 98

Calm or Crazy Coping Skills 99

Coping and Feelings Thermometer 100

Coping and Capable 101

Design Your Own Coping Space 102

Find Your Words 103

Cool and Calm Reminder 104

Bad Day Do-Over 105

Helping Hands 107

I Am Connected 108

On-the-Go Calming Kit 109

Mindful Practice 110

Wave Breathing 111

Mindful Mountain 112

Grounding Scripts 113

Mandala Coloring 114

Mindful Mandala 117

Love Language 118

Daily DJ 119

Mindful Mealtime 120

I Spy with My Five Senses 121

Mindful Minute 122

Chapter 5: Thawing the Freeze: Building Problem-Solving Pathways 125

Mindset Manager 125

Problem-Solving Mindset 126

Mindset Reminders 127

Mindset Jar 128

Problems and Options: Part 1 129

Problems and Consequences: Part 2 131

Decision Making 133

Marvelous Mindset 134

Marvelous Mindset in Action 135

Problem-Solving Scenarios 137

Problem-Responding Worksheet 139

Calm and Relaxed Think Sheet 141

Coping with Change 142

Making a Back-Up Plan 143

One Foot Forward 144

Eek! I'm Trying Something New and Different 145

Trying Something New 146

Making a Change 148

Owning Our Choices 150

Chapter 6: Fostering Empowerment and Self-Care 151

Discovering My Inner Self 151

Who Am I? 152

My Highlight Reel 153

Real Reel vs. Highlight Reel 154

Self-Awareness: What's Important? 155

Self-Acceptance: I Love ME! 156

Empowerment 157

Just Right Communication: Take 1 158

Just Right Communication: Take 2 159

What Type of Communicator Am I? 160

Making an Impression 162

All About Me 164

Taking Care of Myself and Others 165

What Is Self-Care? 166

How Do You Self-Care? 167

Self-Care for the Senses 169

Self-Care Challenge 170

Unplugging to Recharge 172

Mundane to Meaningful 173

Thanking the Stars 174

"Me Time" Schedule 175

You Are Loved 176

References **177**

Introduction

One day at school, Jasmine, 12 years old, came across two boys play-fighting in the hallway. Several peers walked past, ignoring their behavior, but Jasmine had a very different reaction. What she saw triggered memories of past experiences of violence and uncertainty, and it caused her to fear for her safety. Suddenly her heart began to race, she started sweating and breathing heavily, and she felt the need to escape. Without understanding why, Jasmine knew she had to get away, and she ran to hide in the bathroom. Unable to find the words to tell others about her concerns, she cowered in the bathroom hoping her fears would subside. She felt frozen and didn't know how to manage the waves of emotion washing over her. It just felt easier to hide. The domestic violence she had experienced—which no one else was aware of—had limited her ability to trust adults, make friends, and problem solve when faced with environmental, social, and psychological triggers.

Jasmine is far from alone in her daily quest to maintain basic needs, such as safety, trust, and personal connection. In fact, research suggests over 45 percent of children across the United States have been exposed to at least one adverse or traumatic experience during their lifetime.[1] Adverse childhood experiences refer to traumatic events or states of living that disrupt a child's ability to develop healthy emotions and relationships. Examples include any kind of abuse, neglect, domestic violence, or family disruptions (like divorce or loss of a family member) to name a few. Significant events like global crises, can also create instability and economic stress which can drastically disrupt familiar routines (e.g. school, access to basic necessities) and connections with trusted peers and adults. If left untreated or unresolved, these adverse experiences negatively impact health, increase the risk of drug addiction, and greatly impact children's success in the future.[2]

Defining Traumatic Experiences

Trauma, adverse childhood experiences, and toxic stress are all terms used to describe developmental disruptions or experiences that can overwhelm children's ability to cope and interfere with their growth and development. While these experiences are traditionally viewed as a single event, stressful events and circumstances can vary in situation and chronicity (e.g., ongoing financial issues, health problems, or mental health issues). Each person's experience is also dependent on their innate capacity to cope, their support network, and other environmental factors.

	Definition
Trauma	The Substance Abuse and Mental Health Services Administration (SAMSHA) describes trauma as the result of "an event, series of events, or set of circumstances experienced by an individual as physically or emotionally harmful or life-threatening with lasting adverse effects on the individual's functioning and mental, physical, social, emotional, or spiritual well-being."[3]
Adverse Childhood Experiences	The Center for Disease Control (CDC) describes adverse childhood experiences as "potentially traumatic events that occur in childhood (0-17 years) such as experiencing violence, abuse, or neglect; witnessing violence in the home; and having a family member attempt or die by suicide. Also included are aspects of the child's environment that can undermine their sense of safety, stability, and bonding such as growing up in a household with substance misuse, mental health problems, or instability due to parental separation or incarceration of a parent, sibling, or other member of the household."[4]
Toxic Stress	Toxic stress refers to the "prolonged activation of stress response systems in the absence of protective relationships"[5] and these experiences can be "extreme, long-lasting, and severe."[6]

For children and adolescents living and coping with adversities from their past, even normal, everyday challenges can be perceived as threats, which results in the activation of their primal fight, flight, or freeze responses. These primal responses can manifest in many ways: from the explosive child who reacts instantly at minor setbacks to the fearful adolescent who refuses to leave their parent due to concerns about safety. Exposure to trauma, stress, and pain can inhibit children's abilities to problem solve, which leaves survival thinking as their only course.

So what can we do? There is no form of bubble wrap strong enough to protect or undo past traumatic experiences. However, children can shield themselves and bounce back from adversity if their social-emotional capacities are developed and supported. These social-emotional skills include relationship building, emotion regulation, problem solving, and empowerment. In order to heal, children need opportunities to build healthy relationships with peers and adults, to find ways to make emotions more manageable, and to develop effective social language and self-advocacy skills. That is where this book can help: It provides children with the tools needed to develop strong social-emotional skills so they can overcome these adverse experiences.

Who Is This Book For?

This workbook is designed for professionals working with children and adolescents who are living with or learning to move forward from life's difficulties. It is applicable to a wide range of professionals, including psychologists, counselors, social workers, behavioral specialists, occupational therapists, and speech and language pathologists. Geared toward clients ages 10 and older (who can more readily express their thoughts with the guidance and support of a clinician), this workbook provides activities to help professionals engage children and tap into their innate capacity for resiliency. As professionals, we play a powerful role in helping build the bridge for recovery and a positive future.

What Is In This Book?

This workbook is designed to validate children's experiences and to move them toward a path that allows them to be successful in the future. Built on key tenets of trauma-informed care—safety, trust, choice, collaboration, and empowerment[7]—this workbook provides compassionate and relevant activities to support the healing process. Additionally, this toolbox aims to support the social-emotional processes that are disrupted by adverse or traumatic events that occur during early development. By addressing adversity through a trauma-informed approach, clinicians and caregivers can promote social-emotional growth and help children reestablish a sense of safety, routine, and connection.

Elements of a Trauma-Informed Approach

- Reaffirming safety

- Building trust

- Developing empathy and compassion

- Exploring experiences, impacts, and fears

- Validating feelings

- Tailoring strategies to support self-regulation and self-awareness

- Developing problem-solving pathways to ensure success

- Supporting self-empowerment

In the following chapters, you'll find activities for clients and families to reestablish or increase feelings of safety and trust, address cognitive distortions, foster healthy relationships, learn healthy problem-solving pathways, and build self-efficacy. Each activity was developed using a collaborative perspective, incorporating elements of psychology and speech and language pathology. The following activities are included:

- **Client activities and worksheets** are created for children to complete themselves within the session or as homework. Caregivers are invited to review the activities with their children so they can gain insight on new skills and help carry over newly learned skills.

- **Caregiver activities and worksheets** are intended to give caregivers insight on the trauma-informed approach, offer structured activities to engage with their child, and provide extension activities to help children apply skills at home. Other activities are designed to encourage caregivers to gain perspective regarding their own expectations and to facilitate strategies to support their child's positive social-emotional growth.

- **In-session activities** are designed for the clinician to use with the client. Often, the activities require clinical insight and are structured in nature so the clinician can support the client in navigating challenging concepts.

Given that one size does not fit all, this workbook contains a variety of different activities that are intended to meet the needs of a diverse range of clients, which will allow you to address the impact of trauma, no matter the size or scope. Although this workbook is designed to support clients in developing social-emotional skills, it is not a treatment manual. Rather, it is intended to facilitate conversation, supplement your treatment goals, build capacities, encourage carryover in the home setting, and enhance social-emotional skills.

This workbook is broken down into six different chapters, each of which provides you with tools to enhance communication, relationships, self-regulation, and self-advocacy:

Chapter 1: Recognizing Trauma and Moving Forward. These initial activities provide psychoeducation for clients and caregivers by helping them explore the meaning of trauma, chronic stress, and adversity. Clients will have opportunities to address their own fears, to develop tools to help express their needs, and to brainstorm methods to maintain safety when faced with threatening thoughts or events. This chapter also offers tools to help clients survey the personal impact of trauma and stress on their relationships and social-emotional functioning. The tools in this chapter are intended to help clients:

- Understand typical social-emotional development and disruptions
- Define trauma and stress
- Focus on the subjective experience, not the event
- Find safe ways to talk about personal experiences
- Process significant memories or events

Chapter 2: Creating a Foundation of Safety. Many of us take feeling safe and secure for granted, not realizing how essential safety is in order to participate in experiences that grow our knowledge, friendships, and ability to handle life's challenges. Those who have experienced trauma have more difficulty establishing feelings of safety and security, so they must be guided in establishing effective parameters for a "safe environment." They must learn to recognize their emotions and develop a safe place where they can reflect on worries, fears, and reactions to stress. The tools in this chapter are intended to help clients:

- Identify protective and risk factors
- Understand personal triggers and responses to stress
- Define a safety network
- Increase predictability and routine when possible

Chapter 3: Building Trust and Understanding. This chapter explores the concept of building and maintaining trust within a relationship. In order to establish trust with others, children must feel a sense of safety and connection. When navigating relationships, it is essential to find purpose within a variety of personal connections, to recognize and set boundaries, and to allow opportunities for vulnerability. Exploring these ideas will build overall self-awareness and foster a sense of self-control. Furthermore, differentiating levels of trust will help clients establish clear expectations for those around them so they can maintain a safe and trusting social circle where they feel empowered to flourish. The tools in this chapter are intended to help clients:

- Discuss what trust looks and sounds like

- Create a supportive network of trusted individuals

- Accept that it's okay to make mistakes

- Learn to be humble

Chapter 4: From Reliving to Relieving: Self-Regulation Strategies. This chapter focuses on addressing the inner fight, flight, or freeze response and increasing the client's window of tolerance for stress. Clients will have opportunities to identify unhelpful reactions to stress and to develop skills to manage their emotional and physical responses. Activities will engage clients, therapists, and caregivers in recognizing reactions to stressors, identifying healthy coping mechanisms, and developing a "bag of tricks" to cope with future challenges. The tools in this chapter are intended to help clients:

- Manage big, intense emotions in safe ways

- Explore coping skills to determine what works best

- Recognize trusted individuals who can support coping strategies

- Be present and grounded in the moment

Chapter 5: Thawing the Freeze: Building Problem-Solving Pathways. This chapter addresses the "frozen" moment children and adolescents run into when faced with a range of problems (*Ahh! I have a problem! The sky is falling!*). Understanding the scope of a problem, mapping out different responses, and being able to prioritize tasks are essential components of problem solving. Activities include individual worksheets, scenarios, and charts to highlight ways to solve problems effectively. The tools in this chapter are intended to help clients:

- Identify a calm problem-solving mindset

- Understand and predict possible outcomes to situations

- Strengthen decision-making skills

- Learn to cope with changes to routines and to try new things

Chapter 6: Fostering Empowerment and Self-Care. Living in a state of fear and worry can take a toll on a child's self-concept. This chapter provides several tools to foster empowerment and self-agency. Activities focus on identifying personal strengths, building self-esteem, and helping clients find their voice. A variety of self-care activities are also included to support clients and caregivers alike in building in time to nurture their bodies and minds. The tools in this chapter are intended to help clients:

- Recognize their personal strengths and uniqueness
- Build confidence in communicating with others
- Enhance their ability to make their voice heard
- Develop strategies for self-care, wellness, and resiliency

Journey Ahead

Now it is time to commence the journey toward building social-emotional strength. This path may take different directions depending on your client's needs, so use your clinical and ethical judgment when integrating these activities into your practice. By using a trauma-informed approach, you are working toward developing a safe and trusting environment where your client can address triggers and challenges, and work toward a healthier life.

CHAPTER ONE

Recognizing Trauma and Moving Forward

Recognizing Trauma

Our lives are shaped by experiences: the good, the bad, and the challenging. Generally, when life goes "off script" and disruptions occur, we can rebound with the right supports, such as a healthy family network, supportive friends, and well-developed coping skills. However, when disruptions result in significant change, create feelings of uncertainty, or result in ongoing stress, they can be considered traumatic. Because the experience of trauma is subjective, it is often an individual's *responses* to these events—more so than the triggering event itself—that influences whether these disruptions will leave a deeper impact on their life.

In the activities ahead, clients and caregivers can learn about typical development of social-emotional skills and the importance of connection, trust, emotion, and self-regulation. Other activities help introduce the concept of trauma and chronic stress, as well as the disruptions or changes that can occur following traumatic experiences. These activities help create an understanding of common reactions to trauma and facilitate a sharing of personal experiences. These exercises are aimed at helping clients create a dialogue about their experiences in a safe, non-threating manner.

Social-Emotional Checklist

· ·

A child is shaped by a combination of biological and environmental factors that form their beliefs regarding connection, safety, and acceptance that drive the development of social-emotional abilities. Below is a brief summary of basic skills at different stages of life. Can you add a memory or recall a time when your child expressed these skills? Review the lists for the stages of development and do the following:

➢ Place a checkmark by milestones that show trust or connection with others

➢ Circle milestones that show emotional development

➢ Underline milestones that show self-awareness or independence

Babies and Toddlers

- Recognize faces and mimic expressions

- Co-regulate emotions through the caregiver

- Feel safe through consistent caregiver responses

- Learn to follow simple rules and routines as toddlers

- Show signs of independence (toileting, eating, dressing) as toddlers

- Begin to engage in imaginative play as toddlers

Share your memory:

_____

_____

_____

Elementary-Age Children

- Begin to form peer groups

- Are able to identify emotions and express a range of feelings

- Learn to connect actions with consequences

- Engage in independent problem solving

- Begin engaging in perspective-taking and exhibiting empathy toward others

- Become capable of independent decision making

Share your memory:

_____

_____

_____

Teen Years and Onward

- Begin to be more self-aware

- Learn critical problem-solving skills

- Rely heavily on friends for support rather than family

- Develop a unique identity

- Engage in goal setting

- Develop self-reflection abilities

Share your memory:

_____

_____

_____

Client Worksheet

Social-Emotional Shield

· ·

Think of social-emotional skills as natural shields that can help you battle daily challenges and give you the confidence you need to handle the big stuff. Each shield is made up of a set of skills that help you process feelings, connect with others, solve problems, and build self-confidence. Complete this activity by labeling each shield with one of the four labels provided. Then, color your strongest shield, your area of strength.

Shield Labels:

Emotion Regulation   Problem Solving   Connection   Empowerment

Helps you to:
Have self-confidence
Recognize your strengths
Have self-esteem

Helps you to:
Analyze situations
Generate solutions
Set goals

Helps you to:
Recognize and express emotions
Identify triggers
Exhibit self-control

Helps you to:
Trust others
Develop healthy relationships
Respect others

Helpful or Harmful Stress

. . . .

Stress is not always a bad thing. For example, helpful stress can motivate us to work harder, run faster, or focus on a project to finish it on time. Brief moments of stress can motivate us through daily challenges. On the other hand, too much stress can be harmful because it sends us into a constant fight, flight, or freeze mode. When we experience ongoing or chronic stress, it can negatively impact our mental health and possibly damage our physical health.

Helpful Stress

- Increases your attention

- Helps you tackle daily tasks

- Energizes you

- Helps you perform to the best of your abilities

Harmful Stress

- Makes it difficult to focus

- Can make you feel "prickly" or on edge

- Causes changes in appetite and sleep

- Weakens your ability to fight off germs

The following are all examples of situations that could cause stress. Circle situations that could result in **helpful** types of stress, and cross out those that could result in **harmful** types of stress.

- Moving to a new house

- Giving a speech in front of your class

- Struggling with sleep problems

- Living in an unsafe community

- Performing on stage

- Living with a caregiver who is very sick

- Being bullied at school

- Having to take care of siblings

One Step Further: What do you do to fight stress at home or at school? Who do you reach out to for help? _____

_____

Stress and the Brain

· ·

Stress is the brain's natural response to danger, small or large, in the environment. When a stressful event occurs, the brain responds by activating the fight, flight, or freeze response, resulting in a release of stress hormones that sends the body into high alert until the danger is gone. This causes breathing and heart rate to increase, muscles to tighten, and senses to heighten. These changes serve to energize the body and increase alertness to deal with the threat ahead by confronting it head on (fight), running away (flight), or hiding (freeze). When the perceived danger subsides, the body calms and recovers.

Stress impacts everyone differently. Complete this scale to describe times when you felt low, medium, and high levels of stress, and also describe differences in how your body felt at each level. Complete the activity individually or with your caregiver in order to gain an understanding of how different types of stress impact us.

	What are some examples of events that cause you stress?	What does this type of stress feel like in your body? (e.g., heartbeat, breathing, muscles, thoughts)
High Stress		
Medium Stress		
Low Stress		

In-Session Activity

Life Stressors and Control

. . . .

Brief, yet impactful, events, like being in a car accident or surviving a hurricane that devastated a town, can cause sudden life changes that are outside your control. Other long-term events that are out of your control—like parent divorce, loss of a loved one, deployment, or serious, ongoing situations, like neglect or entering the foster care system—can also significantly disrupt social-emotional development. Review the stressful examples in the chart provided, and mark if they are in your control or out of your control. Then, shade in the events that would be problematic for you.

In	Out	Life Stressor
		Experiencing a natural disaster
		Living with a family member who has physical or mental health issues
		Needing to make new friends because you moved for your parent's job
		Experiencing the death of a family member
		Preparing for an upcoming test at school
		Having a parent get deployed
		Reaching out to an adult for help when you need it
		Add your own:
		Add your own:

Recognizing Trauma and Adversity

. . . .

Disruptive life events can be serious and devasting but not necessarily traumatic. These events, whether they are short-lived or ongoing, become traumatic when the person views the situation as such. That is, trauma is a *subjective* experience because it is individual to the person's experience. Trauma can happen to someone who is directly involved in the disruptive event or to someone who witnessed the event happen. This exercise will help you identify different types of events that could potentially be considered traumatic, as well as whether these events could cause short-term or long-lasting disruptions.

Step 1: In the boxes below, list examples of events that could be considered adverse, traumatic, or seriously stressful in your personal life, family life, and community. You can write your own examples or use the examples provided.

Examples: *A robbery in the community, the death of a caregiver, chronic illness, witnessing a violent tornado in the community, homelessness, a parent losing their job, being a victim of neglect or abuse, or living in an unsafe community.*

Personal Events	Family Events	Community Events

Step 2: Label whether each type of event listed below is short-lived, ongoing, or both.

_____ Being in a car accident

_____ Having a serious, ongoing illness

_____ Losing a caregiver

_____ Experiencing a hurricane

_____ Witnessing a crime in the community

_____ Living in poverty

Short-Term vs. Ongoing Stress

Some disruptive experiences can cause temporary pain and stress, while some experiences are ongoing and can create constant stress. Stressful events are *manageable* when they result in low to moderate stress and are challenging but temporary. However, these events become *problematic* if they result in significant or ongoing life disruption and cause higher levels of stress. As you know, too much stress can be harmful. Significant or ongoing stress can change all aspects of your daily life. In this activity, you'll think about how stress can impact your mental and physical well-being.

Part 1: On the left-hand side, draw your mind in a calm, low stress way. On the right-hand side, draw your mind in a very stressed way!

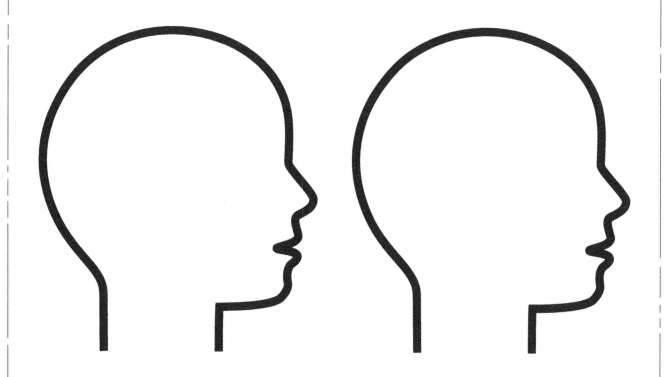

Part 2: How can very high levels of stress impact your body, mind, and emotions? Working with a clinician or trusted adult, brainstorm ways stress can impact you in each of the categories listed.

	Short-Term Stress	Ongoing Stress
Physical Well-Being (Eating, sleeping, health, exercise)		
Emotional Well-Being (Moods, ability to adapt to change, ability to express emotions)		
Relationships (Trust, how you interact with others, how often you seek out others)		
Problem-Solving Skills (Ability to predict what might happen, decision-making skills)		
Self-Concept (Belief in yourself, self-image, self-confidence)		

Creating Conversation

It can be challenging for children to recall or explain emotional memories due to the stress they cause, and they often lack order for this very reason as well. The following activities can be used to help children start a conversation about the life events they have experienced—the good and not so good times, traumatic or not. The initial activities assist clients in creating a broader emotional vocabulary, whereas subsequent activities focus on identifying important memories and sequencing events. Children can create a timeline to show life events that have led up to the present day and then create a future timeline showcasing their individual strengths and goals.

Client Worksheet

Calm Words Cloud

· ·

Words can be hard to find, sort, or express when you are filled with emotions or stress. Although it's sometimes easier to stick with simple words like *okay*, *fine*, or *good* to describe how you are feeling, these words don't have enough detail to describe what's really going on inside. In contrast, words like *relaxed*, *peaceful*, or *quiet* can help paint a clearer picture of how you are feeling. To help generate words that describe different moods, use this activity to create a word cloud. Fill in the clouds with words, places, feelings, or people that describe "calm" to you. Use pictures, colors, or patterns—like polka dots or stripes—to express yourself.

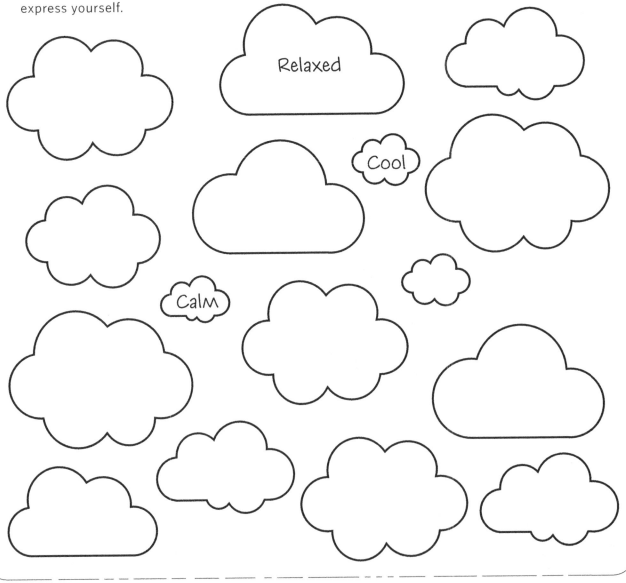

Client Worksheet

Word Storm

· · · · · · · · · · · · · · · · · · ·

Now that you've identified some words associated with a sense of calm, brainstorm some words that you associate with stress, fear, or troubling times. Think about any words, places, feelings, or people that describe these experiences—and fill in the shapes here to express yourself.

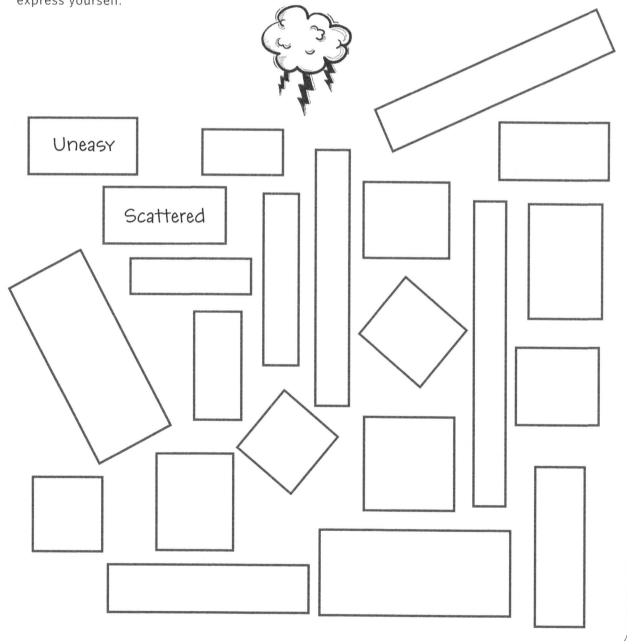

Uneasy

Scattered

Memories and Feelings

· ·

Talking about memories helps to tell our story. Certain memories, like going to your first baseball game or baking with a favorite relative, can create warm feelings and remind you of your connection to others. Other memories may cause you to feel unhappy or uncomfortable. Those memories are just as important but may be more difficult to talk about. For this activity, think about some memories that help tell your story. Start by listing your favorite memories at the top. Describe the memory or write key words that can help you describe what occurred. As you work your way down the list, end with memories that are more difficult or emotional. These are important too! When you are done, go back and add details, like when the event occurred, who was around, and where it happened.

1. _____

_____

2. _____

_____

3. _____

_____

4. _____

_____

5. _____

_____

Part 1: Then and Now Icons

. . . .

Our lives are influenced by relationships, family events, good memories, and other events that might be harder to share. Using the spaces provided, draw or write down events that tell your story. What events or changes can you remember? Use some (or all) of the icons provided or add some of your own.

Important Personal or Family Events (e.g., birth, marriage, divorce, moving, new job)

Special or Important Relationships (e.g., family members, friends, neighbors, coaches)

Sad Events (e.g., loss of a loved one, personal event, family event)

Change Events (e.g., moving, starting a new school, family change like deployment)

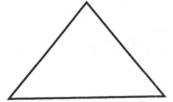 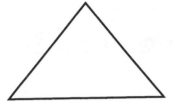 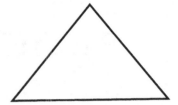

Favorite Times (e.g., favorite memories or experiences)

Client Worksheet

Then and Now Timeline
· ·

Once you have created your icons, place them on the timeline listed here, or make your own timeline on a larger piece of paper. Timelines help create a visual representation of events, emotional memories, and relationships that can be hard to talk about or recall in order. Be sure to include events like births, family events, personal events, and even friend events.

Now

Then

Part 2: Now and Beyond Icons

· ·

You have finished your timeline of your past, so now let's look toward the future. Brainstorm what you'd like your life to look like. As you venture into your future, what goals do you have? What supportive relationships will help you reach your dreams and aspirations? What strengths do you possess to help you get there?

Personal Strengths (e.g., school subjects, problem-solving skills, patience, being a good friend)

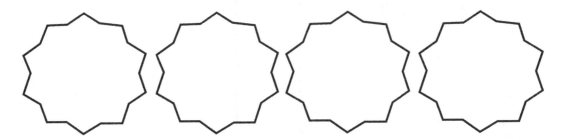

Personal Goals (e.g., what you would like to accomplish soon and in the future)

| In 1 month... | In 1 year... | In 10 years... |

Supportive Relationships (e.g., important family, friends, caregivers)

Client Worksheet

Now and Beyond Timeline

· ·

While you may be working through some difficult times, your story has just begun. Brainstorm what you would like your future to look like. What goals and dreams do you have? Place your Now and Beyond Icons on the timeline below, or make your own timeline on a larger piece of paper.

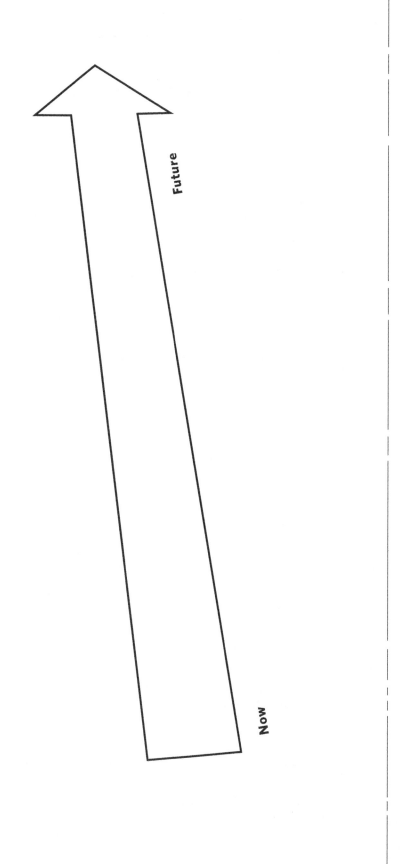

Future

Now

What Happened?

· ·

Finding words to describe distressing events can be challenging. This clinician tool can be used in session to support clients, as it provides a visual aid to guide conversations and allows clients to more easily share their perspective. When conversations are limited or difficult, encourage clients to use the scales here to express their experiences.

What happened to you? Describe the distressing event(s): _____

_____

_____

_____

_____

_____

_____

_____

_____

How long did the event(s) last?

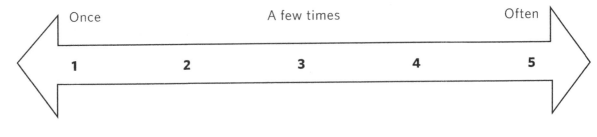

Once		A few times		Often
1	2	3	4	5

How much notice did you have before the event occurred?

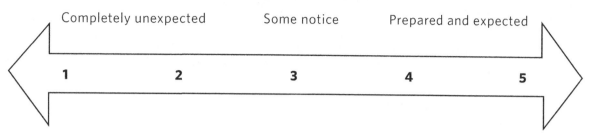

Completely unexpected   Some notice   Prepared and expected

1   2   3   4   5

How much personal stress did the event cause?

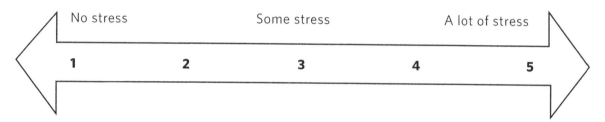

No stress   Some stress   A lot of stress

1   2   3   4   5

How much family stress did the event cause?

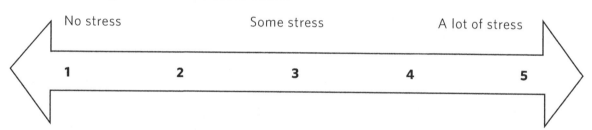

No stress   Some stress   A lot of stress

1   2   3   4   5

How much change did the event cause?

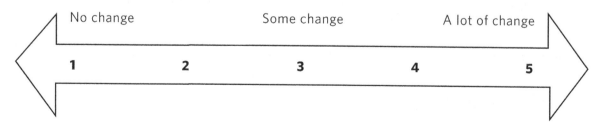

No change   Some change   A lot of change

1   2   3   4   5

What is Bothering Me?

. . . .

If it is difficult for clients to find the words to describe what is bothering them, you can use the scales here to help them describe their experience. First, ask clients to write down what is bothering them. If it is hard to describe the events, then use the scales below to help them communicate how they feel about their problems.

My problem: _____

_____

_____

How big is your problem?

No problem	Small problem	I'm not sure	Big problem	Major problem
1	2	3	4	5

How urgent is your problem?

Not urgent	It can wait	I'm not sure	I need help soon	Emergency
1	2	3	4	5

How does it make you feel?

Very Comfortable	Comfortable	Okay	Uncomfortable	Very Uncomfortable
1	2	3	4	5

Do you feel safe?

Very Safe	Safe	Okay	Unsafe	Very Unsafe
1	2	3	4	5

In My Own Words

. . . .

Unfortunately, upsetting or troubling events can be part of your life story. Describe what happened to you below with as many details as you are comfortable. Answer the following questions to help provide more details about your experience. When you are finished, share your story with your clinician or a trusted adult.

What happened to you?

_____

_____

_____

_____

_____

_____

_____

_____

_____

When did it happen?

Today   A year ago

Yesterday   Other: _____

A month ago

How did you feel?

Upset	Scared	Sad	Ashamed	Worried	Hurt
Embarrassed	Alone	Anxious	Unsafe	Other: _____	

What feelings were manageable? _____

_____

_____

_____

Were any feelings overwhelming? _____

_____

_____

_____

Did anyone help you?

Caregiver   School

Sibling   Police Officer

Relative   Other: _____

Friend

How do you feel now?

I can handle it   I need some help   I really need help

Moving Forward

In this section, the client and caregiver will work together to identify areas for social-emotional growth and recovery. Activities are intended to help children uncover feelings that may be less obvious to others, to provide caregivers a way to describe their concerns, and to offer opportunities for clients and caregivers to reflect on areas of social-emotional growth. Additionally, there are goal-setting activities that can be used to help guide and target areas of growth, such as developing trust, managing feelings, problem solving, and empowerment.

Fight, Flight, or Freeze Feelings

· ·

Understanding how behaviors and symptoms impact your child's performance is an initial step in problem solving and skill building. This activity will help you target areas of concern and help guide further planning for social-emotional growth.

What are the major behaviors or symptoms your child is presenting with? Write individual responses, or select from the chart provided:

_____

_____

_____

_____

_____

Fight Examples	Flight Examples	Freeze Examples
• Argumentative	• Avoiding others	• Withdrawn
• Impulsive	• Restless	• Numb
• Defiant	• Inattentive	• Inattentive
• Inattentive	• Scared	• Worried
• Lacking self-control	• Worried	• Stuck
• Agitated	• Jumpy	• Obsessive
• Quick to react	• Disorganized	• Non-responsive

These behaviors might really be saying:

- I see this situation or person as a threat.

- I don't feel safe.

- I am not sure I can trust you.

- My emotions are dangerous.

- I am worried about what might happen.

- I can't solve this problem.

- Others don't understand what I am going through.

Place a checkmark where your child may be having difficulty.

	Home	School	Other: _____
Feelings of Safety			
Developing Trust			
Emotion Regulation			
Problem Solving			
Belief in Self			

My Iceberg of Feelings

· ·

What people see on the outside does not always match what you are experiencing on the inside. Other people may notice how you behave, how your body responds (with tears, laughter, or yelling), or how you interact with others (by engaging with others a lot or not at all). But what is really going on underneath the surface? Events, circumstances, or other hidden issues can make you feel stuck in survival mode—that is, in a state of fight, flight, or freeze. Use this guide to start the discussion about what elements in your life are causing you stress, where it is happening, and what you are experiencing.

What do others see?

- My behaviors
- My body responses
- My interactions with others

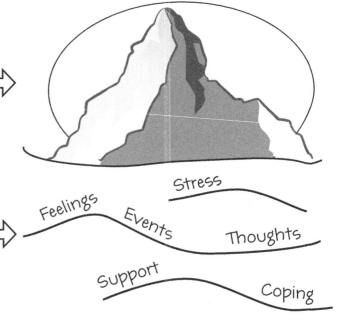

What is really going on with me?

- Holding in my feelings
- Stress at home, in my family, or in my community
- Recurring thoughts or fears

Feelings   Events   Stress   Thoughts   Support   Coping

What are you having difficulty with? Circle the issues you are having trouble with, including what other people can and cannot see.

Fight Examples	Flight Examples	Freeze Examples

• Arguing with peers or adults
 	
• Feeling on edge
 	
• Being easily agitated
 	
• Being quick to react
 	
• Feeling overly aware of your surroundings (e.g., noises, people)
 	
• Other: _____
  _____
 	
• Other: _____
  _____
	• Avoiding others
	
	• Feeling restless
	
	• Feeling inattentive
	
	• Feeling scared
	
	• Feeling worried
	
	• Feeling disorganized
	
	• Other: _____
	  _____
	
	• Other: _____
	  _____
		• Feeling numb
		
		• Lacking focus
		
		• Lacking motivation
		
		• Feeling stuck
		
		• Having recurring thoughts or fears
		
		• Other: _____
		  _____
		
		• Other: _____
		  _____

Where are these issues happening?

☐ At home   ☐ At school   ☐ Other: _____

Child Readiness Check-In

· ·

Many activities in this book require participation between a child and a trusted adult, whether it be a caregiver or clinician. Taking a trauma-informed approach can mean that interactions have to wait until everyone is physically and mentally prepared to participate. When considering whether to work on a new coping skill, discuss events at school, or address an important matter, it is necessary to think about what true readiness looks like. Using the following checklist, take stock of your child's facial expressions, body language, and voice to determine if they are ready to talk.

Child Readiness Signs	Ready to Talk?
What does my child's face look like? ❑ Looking at me ❑ Calm ❑ No tension ❑ Smile/neutral expression ❑ Other: _____	❑ Yes ❑ No
What is my child's body language? ❑ Relaxed, no tension ❑ Sitting or standing calmly, not pacing ❑ Quiet hands/feet (no tapping) ❑ Other: _____	❑ Yes ❑ No
What does my child sound like? ❑ Normal volume (no yelling) ❑ Easy to understand (not speaking too quickly) ❑ Tone of voice is calm, engaged, reasonable ❑ Other: _____	❑ Yes ❑ No

Caregiver Readiness Check-In

· ·

Evaluating your own readiness to engage in a trauma-informed conversation is just as important as evaluating your child's readiness to do so. Once you have assessed your child's readiness signs, take stock of your own facial expressions, body language, and voice. Evaluate your emotional readiness to have a positive conversation with your child.

Caregiver Readiness Signs	Ready to Talk?
What does my face look like? ❑ Calm ❑ No tension ❑ Smile/neutral expression ❑ Other: _____	❑ Yes ❑ No
What is my body language? ❑ No tension ❑ Sitting or standing calmly ❑ Quiet hands/feet (no tapping) ❑ Other: _____	❑ Yes ❑ No
What does my voice sound like? ❑ Normal volume (no yelling) ❑ Easy to understand (not speaking too quickly) ❑ Tone of voice is calm, engaged, reasonable ❑ Other: _____	❑ Yes ❑ No
Am I emotionally ready to have a positive conversation with my child?	❑ Yes ❑ No

Social-Emotional Skills Inventory

· ·

Use this inventory to highlight your child's strengths and weaknesses. There are no right or wrong answers. Rate each area on a scale of 1 (*easy*) to 5 (*very hard*). Use your ratings to guide goal-setting activities in this section.

Developing Trust: How does your child do with...

Connecting with others?	1	2	3	4	5
Creating friendships with peers?	1	2	3	4	5
Maintaining friendships?	1	2	3	4	5
Understanding others?	1	2	3	4	5

Managing Feelings: How does your child do with...

Recognizing their own feelings?	1	2	3	4	5
Managing big feelings?	1	2	3	4	5
Identifying helpful coping skills?	1	2	3	4	5
Using helpful coping skills?	1	2	3	4	5

Problem Solving: How well does your child...

Solve challenging problems by themselves?	1	2	3	4	5
Identify or find alternative solutions to problems?	1	2	3	4	5
Ask for help when they are stuck?	1	2	3	4	5
Take a risk and try new things?	1	2	3	4	5

Empowerment: How well can your child...

Identify personal strengths?	1	2	3	4	5
Take the perspective of others?	1	2	3	4	5
Make their voice heard?	1	2	3	4	5
Take care of their body and mind?	1	2	3	4	5

Clinician Note: You can use the ratings as a source of information to select areas or activities to promote social-emotional growth.

Social-Emotional Skills Inventory

• •

Make your voice heard! It is important to acknowledge your unique strengths and challenges. Strengths are areas where you feel confident, and challenges are areas where you can improve. Rate each area on a scale of 1 (*easy*) to 5 (*very hard*).

Trust and Safety: How easy is it to…

Trust others?	1	2	3	4	5
Create friendships with peers?	1	2	3	4	5
Maintain friendships?	1	2	3	4	5
Set boundaries with others?	1	2	3	4	5

Managing Feelings: How easy is it to…

Recognize your own feelings?	1	2	3	4	5
Manage big feelings?	1	2	3	4	5
Identify coping skills to help with feelings?	1	2	3	4	5
Use helpful, positive coping skills (e.g., asking for help instead of putting head down)?	1	2	3	4	5

Problem Solving: How easy is it to…

Stick with and solve challenging problems?	1	2	3	4	5
Find alternative solutions to problems?	1	2	3	4	5
Ask for help when you are stuck?	1	2	3	4	5
Try new things?	1	2	3	4	5

Empowerment: How easy is it to…

Consider others' feelings?	1	2	3	4	5
Reflect on your abilities?	1	2	3	4	5
Make your voice heard?	1	2	3	4	5
Take care of your body and mind?	1	2	3	4	5

CHAPTER TWO

Creating a Foundation of Safety

Protective Assets and Risk Factors

Our day-to-day life is influenced by protective and risk factors that make it easier or more difficult to handle stressful problems. Protective factors, like believing in ourselves or having a positive role model, can buffer against the effects of stress and guide us toward positive problem-solving approaches. In contrast, risk factors—such as a lack of positive role models, unhealthy coping skills, and reduced support—can negatively impact our ability to make healthy decisions. Both protective and risk factors exist at the individual level, the family or relationship level, and the community level. The following activities are intended to help children recognize and balance these unique factors.

Client Worksheet

Building Protective Factors

. . . .

Protective factors build a person's ability to handle everyday stressors and process major life challenges. These protective factors—which include individual, peer, home, and community factors—work together like a honeycomb to create a positive buffer. For this activity, use the examples provided to complete the honeycomb by filling in a range of protective factors. You can also brainstorm your own examples to make the honeycomb even stronger.

Examples of protective factors:

- Healthy peer groups
- Being able to problem solve
- Joining a club at school
- Safe living environment

- Supportive parents
- Positive self-esteem
- Healthy eating habits
- Friendly neighborhood

- Being able to make friends
- Welcoming school
- Joining a sports team
- Being able to cope with change

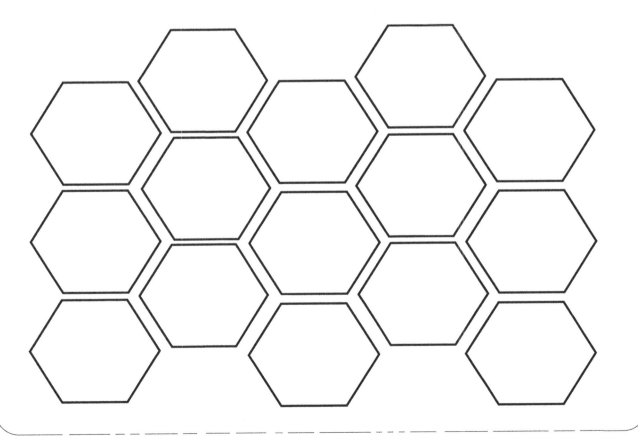

Protective Bubbles

· ·

Hey there, protective factor expert! Now that you can define and recognize protective factors, it's time to explore your own protective makeup. What is in your protective "bubble" that keeps you afloat when times get tough? What is in your inner makeup, family, and community that keeps you focused and headed in a positive direction? What inner abilities do you have that make you strong? Are you flexible, helpful, and caring? What about important relationships? Who do you go to when you need advice, support, or help? Finally, what is unique about your own community at school or in your neighborhood that keeps you connected? Add your own personal factors to the bubbles provided.

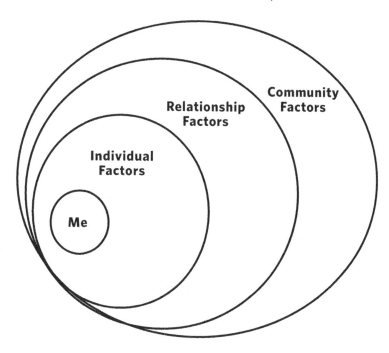

Follow-Up Thoughts:
How do your personal factors, relationships, and connection with your community help you be your best self?

_____

_____

_____

What Are Risks?

. . . .

Think of risks as challenges present in your life. What factors make life more challenging? In this activity, create your own personal definition of "risk" using your senses of sight, sound, and touch. Then, try to think of words or pictures that convey what risk means to you. Finally, practice identifying risks by reading through the examples provided and labeling them as individual, family, or community risks.

Step 1: Define Risk

A risk looks like _____

A risk sounds like _____

A risk feels like _____

A risk is _____

Step 2: Build Your Vocabulary

List three words that are like "risk" (synonyms), or draw what risk looks like to you.

Step 3: Identify Individual, Family, and Community Risks

In the examples provided, circle individual risk factors, place a square around family risk factors, and cross out community risk factors.

Anxiety	Poor academic performance	Uninvolved parents
Divorced parents	Peers who break rules	Health problems
Parent with depression	Feeling lonely	Difficulties making friends
Neighborhood fights	Changing homes frequently	Being bullied by peers

Examining Risks

. . . .

Life is full of risks, from personal factors (like unhealthy habits or anxiety) to community factors (like an unsafe neighborhood or a lack of access to resources). Everyone experiences risks, but having multiple risks increases the chance of engaging in unhealthy or dangerous habits. Use this worksheet to identify your own personal, family, and community risks. Recognizing and acknowledging unhealthy risk factors opens the door to replace those risks with healthier supports.

What is your greatest personal risk?

_____

_____

What is your greatest family or relationship risk?

_____

_____

What is your greatest community risk?

_____

_____

What can you do to reduce your risks?

_____

_____

Who can help you reduce your risks?

_____

_____

Weighing Assets and Risks

. . . .

Use this activity to reflect on your protective assets and risk factors. First, list all the individual, family, and community factors that provide protection for you. Then, identify the personal, family, or community factors that may pose a risk in your life. Discuss your list with your clinician, a trusted adult, or a family member. Circle the protective assets that that help you the most and identify a risk factor you would like to reduce or improve upon.

	Protective Assets	Risk Factors
Individual Factors	<ul><li></li><li></li><li></li><li></li><li></li></ul>	<ul><li></li><li></li><li></li><li></li><li></li></ul>
Relationship Factors	<ul><li></li><li></li><li></li><li></li><li></li></ul>	<ul><li></li><li></li><li></li><li></li><li></li></ul>
Community Factors	<ul><li></li><li></li><li></li><li></li><li></li></ul>	<ul><li></li><li></li><li></li><li></li><li></li></ul>

Identifying Triggers

When people are faced with a situation that makes them uncomfortable or even upset, it can be easy to jump to conclusions or predict the worst possible outcomes. In this case, the mind immediately senses danger, causing the fight, flight, or freeze response to activate until the person feels safe again. But not every challenge or worry is a threat to safety. In fact, most challenges are manageable problems that can be addressed with the right mindset or approach. In this section, children will learn how to identify and navigate their individual triggers, such as memories or situations that make them uncomfortable. What is triggering for one child may not be triggering for another, so helping children gain awareness of their personal triggers can help guide them in using meaningful coping skills to stay in control.

Client Worksheet

Threat, Thought, or Challenge?

· ·

When we're stressed, it can be hard to assess what is a threat, a challenge, or even just a thought. Our bodies and minds can quickly jump into survival mode before we even have a chance to assess the situation. Viewing challenges as threats can make us avoid people, keep us from trying new things, and prevent us from making sensible decisions. In this activity, you'll learn to differentiate between threats, challenges, and thoughts by looking up the definition of each or by creating your own. Then, you'll create or find an image to remind you of each definition. Finally, you'll test your knowledge by identifying examples of threats, challenges, and thoughts.

Definition   **Image Reminder**

Threat: _____

_____

_____

Challenge: _____

_____

_____

Thought: _____

_____

_____

In the statements provided, circle thoughts, cross out possible threats, and place a star next to challenges.

1. I'll never get this done!

2. A tiger is running toward me!

3. I'm moving to a new school.

4. A stranger is knocking at my door.

5. There is a tornado warning.

6. I'll never make tryouts for soccer. Everyone is better than I am.

7. I don't know anyone in my computer class.

8. I have to give a presentation in front of a large group.

9. Making friends is not easy, they will just let me down.

Client Worksheet

Worry Workshop

· ·

Worries are often negative thoughts or expectations we have about ourselves or others. It can involve imagining the worst possible outcome or having negative beliefs about ourselves. Worries or "what-ifs" can increase stress in the body, keep us from trying new things or interacting with others, or simply distract us from daily activities. Use this activity to identify your current or past worries. Then, brainstorm a safety anchor (which can be a helpful item, activity, person, or place) to help you feel grounded when your worry emerges. Finally, replace the worry with a positive thought you can say to yourself to tackle your worry.

Example:

Worry: I worry about sleeping in the dark. I feel unsafe if I can't see.

Safety Anchor: Before I go to bed, I will read a story to quiet my mind. I will also use a small nightlight so it's not so dark.

Positive Thought or Saying: Tomorrow will be good day.

Example:

My Worry: _____

_____

Safety Anchor: _____

_____

Positive Thought or Saying: _____

_____

Example:

My Worry: _____

_____

Safety Anchor: _____

_____

Positive Thought or Saying: _____

_____

What Triggers Your Fear Response?

· ·

When you are faced with a situation that activates your fear response, how do you react? Do you fight, flight, or freeze? With the help of your clinician, examine what types of events trigger your fear response, describe how your body typically reacts, and discuss how you know when the threat is over. This activity is best done in a calm, safe environment. Save this as a reference sheet as you work through later activities to help define triggers and, most importantly, to identify strategies to help you regain control.

	Fight	Flight	Freeze
What "danger" events might cause you to fight, flight, or freeze?			
What does your body look or feel like when this happens?			
How do you know that it is safe again?			

Emotional Triggers or Reminders

. . . .

Each person's emotional triggers are unique. Certain sounds, smells, or places can serve as an emotional reminder of a painful time when you felt unsafe. When you experience these triggers, your mind perceives danger and goes into survival mode. With a trusted adult or clinician, complete the activity to identify your own emotional triggers. Use this activity to guide you in identifying coping skills that can help you maintain feelings of safety.

What types of reminders or triggers cause uncomfortable or unsafe feelings?

Sounds (e.g., loud voices, squealing tires of a car, slamming of a door)

_____

_____

People (e.g., strangers, certain features of individuals)

_____

_____

Places (e.g., specific places or details of uncomfortable places)

_____

_____

Actions (e.g., being unexpectedly touched on the shoulder)

_____

_____

Other Triggers

_____

_____

When I experience an emotional trigger, my typical reaction is to:

_____ Fight

_____ Flight

_____ Freeze

_____ Combination

My body feels like: _____

My brain feels like: _____

Describe your reaction or draw a picture:

Recognizing Triggers, Emotions, and Reactions

· ·

Use this chart to help explore your personal fight, flight, or freeze response. First, describe or draw a time when you were in a calm state, including what emotions you felt, what thoughts you had, and how your body felt. Then, explore times when you reacted in a state of fight, flight, or freeze instead. Notice the differences in thinking and feeling across these different states.

	Calm	Fight	Flight	Freeze
Time				
Emotions				
Thoughts				
Body				

Establishing Safety

Safety is a basic life need in order for individuals to grow and flourish. When children are in an environment that is secure and protected, there is predictability in those who care for them and within their daily routines. For instance, most children don't worry about who is going to be at the bus stop because a familiar caregiver is there every day. After-school routines are well-established, and children "go with the flow." In contrast, children who have experienced trauma may worry about their physical safety, lack consistent emotional support, or experience uncertainty in their daily routines. Caregivers and clinicians can help children reestablish a sense of safety by helping them learn about concepts related to safety, understand triggers that jeopardize personal safety, and learn ways to address those thoughts in a healthy manner. Caregivers can also provide children with the reassurance of safety by establishing and following predictable routines.

Client Worksheet

Safety Pyramid

. . . .

The pyramids weren't built in a day, but in a day, we can build your "pyramid of safety." In this activity, use a variety of colors to indicate different levels of safety. The base of the pyramid should describe the place where you feel the safest. You might write, "I feel the safest with my mom and dad, at home, playing games." As you move higher up the pyramid, you might write, "I feel nervous in a new place, away from my family." Each person's experience is unique, but it is important to be able to express what soothes you and to recognize triggers that endanger your feelings of safety.

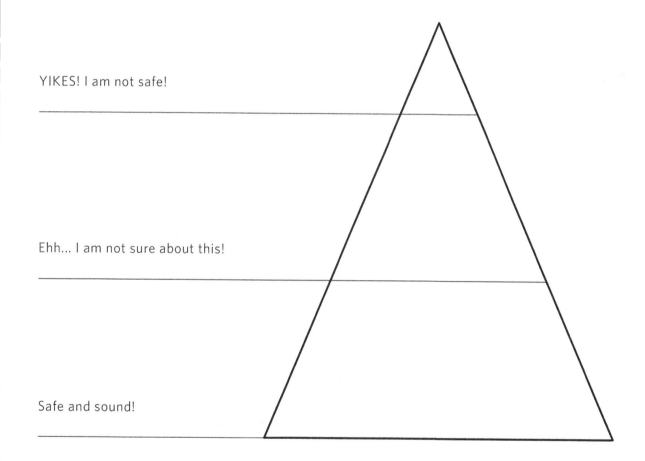

YIKES! I am not safe!

_____

Ehh... I am not sure about this!

_____

Safe and sound!

_____

Setting a Foundation

. . . .

A foundation is the base of a house or building that can support the physical weight of the entire structure. Sounds important, right? We all have a foundation in our lives that helps us handle the "weight" of stress. Our foundation is hard to see but important to identify. Just like the foundation of a building can be composed of bricks, our foundation is made up of our coping skills, our relationships with family and friends, happy memories, peaceful thoughts, and activities that make us happy. What does your foundation look like? Are some spots stronger than others? How can you strengthen your foundation of safety even more?

Thoughts or memories that bring me peace and happiness:

My trusted relationships:

Draw a picture of yourself:

I am good person because:

Coping skills:

How I stay connected (e.g., group activities, sports, clubs, community events):

In-Session Activity

Safe Places, Safe Plans

. . . .

The feeling of being safe can change among settings. Use this worksheet to better define where you feel safe. Then, create a plan in order to increase your feelings of safety in different settings. Complete this activity with the help of a clinician, caregiver, or other trusted adult.

Step 1: List three places where you feel safe.

1. _____ 2. _____ 3. _____

Step 2: Draw yourself in a safe place. Where is it? What does it look like? Who is there?

Step 3: Create a safety plan. Review the variety of settings listed in the chart, and indicate how you can stay safe in each setting and who can help you.

	What can you do?	Who can help you?
At home...		
At school...		
At a friend's house...		
At the playground...		
On the school bus...		
Other: _____		

Safety Gauge

· · · · · · · · · · · · · · · · ·

In this activity, provide examples of what it means to be in the safety zone. You can consider this your home base, where you want to be most of the time. Describe how it looks and feels because this zone is different for everyone. Then, move on to describe the challenge zone and the THREAT! zone. With a trusted adult or clinician, use this tool to talk about different scenarios or real-life experiences for each of these zones. That will help you get a better gauge on what safety, challenge, and threat feel and look like.

Safety Zone:

Example: _____

Looks Like: _____

_____

Feels Like: _____

_____

Challenge Zone:

Example: _____

Looks Like: _____

_____

Feels Like: _____

_____

THREAT! Zone:

Example: _____

Looks Like: _____

_____

Feels Like: _____

_____

In-Session Activity

Safe Feelings

· · · · · · · · · · · · · · · · ·

In order to feel comfortable sharing feelings with our trusted friends and adults, we must understand and believe that our feelings are important and relevant. Sometimes, we can trivialize our emotions and convince ourselves that they don't really matter. We can even feel guilty about how we are feeling, which makes us reluctant to share. In this activity, you will explore your feelings and why they are important to you. This will allow you to feel more confident in sharing all your emotions.

First, describe five different emotions you've had over the past week. Indicate when you felt that way and why the experience is important to you.

I felt...	When...	It's important to me because...

Then, take this page and share it with a trusted friend or adult. Describe your feelings before and after sharing it.

Before	After
• Nervous	• Proud
•	•
•	•
•	•

Comfortable Feelings, Comfortable Me

· ·

As you've been learning, your emotions are a valuable and critical part of who you are. Acknowledging them and their importance helps build your self-worth, self-awareness, and personal safety. Feelings come in all shapes and sizes. Sometimes, feelings can make us comfortable, but other times they can make us uncomfortable—especially when they surprise us or are more intense than expected. In the chart provided, list different emotions that you and your caregiver have felt in the past or currently. Then, provide a personal example or scenario in which the emotion felt comfortable. Finally, challenge yourself to recall a time when it was not so comfortable.

Emotion	Comfortable Situation	Not-So-Comfortable Situation
Happy and excited	Smile and give the teacher a high five after receiving a good grade.	Jump up and yell "Woo hoo!" when you see a good grade on a project.

CHAPTER THREE

Building Trust and Understanding

Building Trust

Trust can be a challenging emotion for children who have experienced trauma. Often, traumatic experiences alter or disrupt the development of trust, so it is important to help repair this element in order to promote recovery. To trust another person means that you have an open relationship with that person, that they have demonstrated trustworthiness to you, and that their actions have proven that they value your well-being. In a truly trusting relationship, people can safely reveal and discuss a range of emotions. These trusted relationships can involve family members, caregivers, friends, and community members.

The activities that follow are intended to help children consider the concept of trust, including how they can develop and build back trust. Given that trust can grow or diminish depending on the actions of others, these tools will help children set clear parameters for their expectations in relationships so they can ensure that they are placing their trust in the most appropriate people. These activities will also provide other people with an opportunity to earn back the child's trust by demonstrating an investment in the child's personal well-being. Understanding that people make mistakes, or that trust can be lost, is essential in creating long-term connections that promote personal growth.

Baseline Trust Profile

· ·

In this activity, create your own definition of trust by describing what trust looks and feels like to you. Use this as a baseline measure of what trust means to you, and revisit this activity as your trust with others increases. Take notice of any changes in this definition across time.

1. Who do you trust?

    Family member(s): _____

    Friend(s): _____

    Community member(s): _____

2. What does trust look like? What personal traits do other people have that resemble trust? For example: being a good listener, being reliable, and being respectful. Draw or describe that here.

3. What does trust sound like? Describe something a person might say to indicate that you can trust them.

    _____

    _____

4. What does trust feel like? Draw a picture of a time when you felt trusted.

Levels of Trust

. . . .

There are different levels of trust among the people in our lives. Some people have earned more trust than others, while some deserve no trust because they are unsafe, unpredictable, or strangers. This activity allows you to determine where the individuals in your life belong on the trust ladder. First, you will develop your own idea bank. List the names of a variety of people in your life, including close friends, acquaintances, teachers, coaches, caregivers, cousins, and social media personalities. Then, create a trust ladder by placing those names into the corresponding trust categories.

Step 1: Create an Idea Bank

Peers	Family Members
1.	1.
2.	2.
3.	3.
School Personnel	**Community Members**
1.	1.
2.	2.
3.	3.
Social Media	**Your Choice!**
1.	1.
2.	2.
3.	3.

Step 2: Develop a Trust Ladder

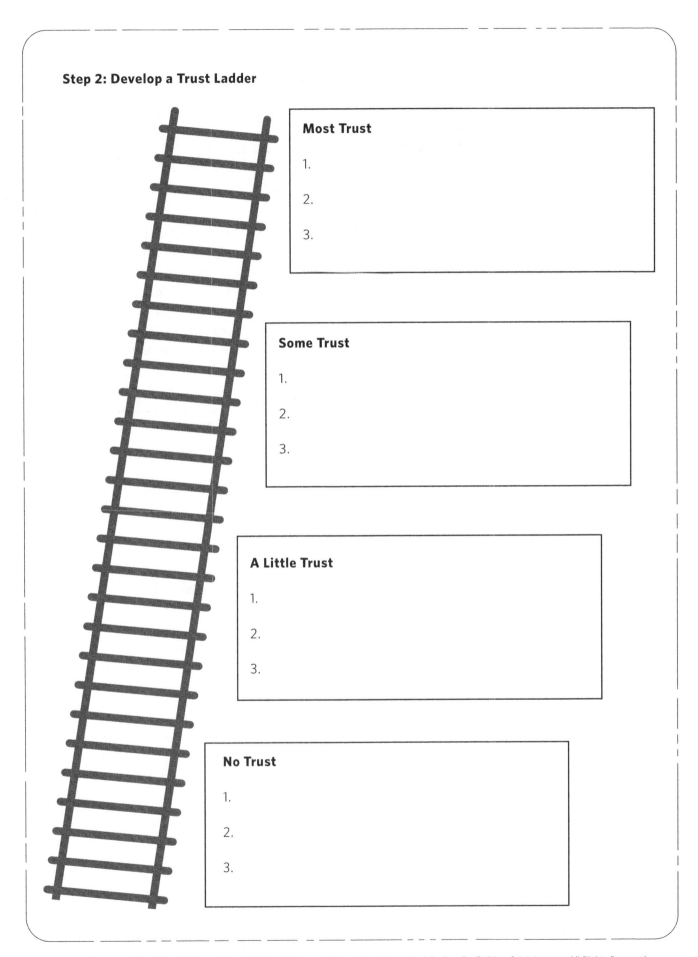

Most Trust

1.

2.

3.

Some Trust

1.

2.

3.

A Little Trust

1.

2.

3.

No Trust

1.

2.

3.

Leveling Up On Trust

· ·

Just because we start off having minimal trust with someone doesn't mean that it must stay that way forever. The people we interact with can move between levels of trust, depending on their behavior. Let's get a specific idea of what it would take to move between levels for you! First, select a starting point and ending point to think about leveling up on trust. For example, you might start with no trust and move up to a little trust. Put a checkmark next to your choice.

I choose…	Starting Point		Ending Point
☐	No Trust	to…	A Little Trust
☐	A Little Trust	to…	Some Trust
☐	Some Trust	to…	Max Trust

Now, reflect on what it would take to move from your starting point to your ending point. For example, if you have someone in the "no trust" category, what would it take to move them into the "a little trust" category? Remember, you can repeat this activity as many times as you would like, looking at different levels of trust.

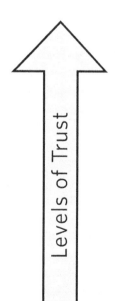

Levels of Trust

Starting Point	Ending Point
My expectation: What *needs* to be done to level up?	The outcome: What *was* done to level up?

Building Back Trust

. . . .

When someone has made a mistake and lost your trust, it is important for you to let them know. It's not always easy to share your feelings with another person, but those tough conversations will ensure that you have strong, authentic relationships. In this activity, identify what action broke your trust, how it made you feel, and how that person can build trust back. After you are done, you can share these answers with that person with the help of a trusted adult or clinician.

When you did...

_____

_____

_____

It made me feel... (use as many words as you want, or you can even draw a picture)

_____

_____

_____

To build back my trust, you can...

1. _____

2. _____

3. _____

Bonus: Turn this activity into a contract by having both you and the other person sign here to agree to work on building back trust.

_____   _____

Making Mistakes

. . . .

Everyone makes mistakes, they are a part of life! Every now and then, though, other people's mistakes can make us lose trust in them. Sometimes, people can rebuild the lost trust. Other times, it is gone for good. This activity will help you set your own boundaries for forgivable or unforgivable mistakes. First, think about some examples when the action of a peer or an adult impacted your ability to trust them. Then, outline those actions and your own feelings in the table provided. Finally, reflect on how long it took you to forgive the person using the following rating scale:

1 = I was only a little upset. It took me a small amount of time to forgive.

2 = I was pretty upset. It took me a medium amount of time to forgive.

3 = I was very upset. It took me a long amount of time to forgive.

4 = I was devastated. I could not forgive this.

What happened?	How did it make you feel?	How long did it take you to forgive them? (1-4 scale)

Reflection:

Your ratings in the final column show you what is forgivable versus unforgivable. A rating of 1-3 means that you were able to move past this event. A rating of 4 means that it broke your trust and is unforgivable. Did you have any experiences that you rated as a 4? What were they?

_____

_____

_____

Creating a Judgment-Free Contract

In order to create an environment of trust and to encourage open discussion, it is essential to have a mutual understanding of the expectations for both the speaker and the listener. This will help everyone feel comfortable and confident when sharing information. The speaker-listener relationship can be between a clinician and a client, between a caregiver and a client, or between a client and another individual. In order to facilitate a productive discussion between the speaker and the listener, both parties should look at the table here and use the checkboxes to indicate which items are important to include in their judgment-free contract. There are also blank spaces where individuals can write in their own specific ideas.

Judgment-Free Contract

When I am speaking...	When I am listening...
☐ I will share information completely.	☐ I will not interrupt.
☐ I will explore my feelings.	☐ I will not judge any feelings or emotions.
☐ I will thoughtfully answer questions.	☐ I will pose relevant questions.
☐ I will not make assumptions about the listener's feelings or emotions.	☐ I will not judge the speaker's experiences.
☐	☐
☐	☐
☐	☐

I agree to be a respectful speaker and listener.

Partner A Name: _____

I agree to be a respectful speaker and listener.

Partner B Name: _____

Clinician Note: This contract can also be used to improve client-caregiver interactions as a carryover activity following a session.

Learning to Be Open

Following a traumatic experience, it is common for children to try to protect themselves by withdrawing to a personal island. On this island, the child will keep their thoughts and feelings to themselves, and won't allow others to come ashore. It's a way to feel insulated and protected, but this strategy prevents them from benefiting from the experiences and knowledge of their trusted peers and adults. By allowing access to their island, children learn to share experiences, receive encouragement and assistance, and support others. Being truly vulnerable means sharing a range of emotions, interactions, and decisions to allow for honest discourse, which will promote self-reflection and self-acceptance. The activities in this section are intended to help children explore letting their guard down and being open, honest, and vulnerable with trusted others. Learning to be open is the first big step in developing positive relationships that nurture personal growth and self-awareness.

Learning to Be Vulnerable

. . . .

Being vulnerable means letting someone you trust see you when you are not at your best, which can make us afraid or nervous. In order to feel comfortable being vulnerable around our trusted friends and adults, we must explore our fear of vulnerability. Think about a time when you were not at your best. Describe it here. Then, explore what you are afraid will happen if you share this information with trusted friends or adults. Next, you will affirm that your trusted friends and adults are here to support you, and you will identify an individual to share your story with. Finally, after sharing your story, come back and reflect on your experience.

1. A time I was not at my best:

_____

_____

2. What am I afraid will happen if I share? That others might see who I am? That others might not accept me?

_____

_____

3. Remember: Our TRUSTED friends and adults always have our best interests in mind. They want to help, not judge. Consider sharing your story with someone you TRUST.

4. How comfortable were you sharing your story?

Very comfortable   Okay   Uncomfortable

5. How empowered do you feel to share your stories with trusted friends or adults?

Very much   Somewhat   Not at all

In-Session Activity

Empowered to Be Vulnerable

· ·

As you have learned, being open to sharing your thoughts, feelings, and experiences requires feelings of trust and safety. However, the reality is that we may not always feel ready for the vulnerability that comes from open and honest communication. This check-in tool can be used to evaluate how prepared you feel to participate in an authentic discussion. Remember, there is no wrong answer here. It is simply a way to gauge how safe you feel in this environment.

> I am in a safe, trusting environment, and I
> can share my thoughts, feelings, and worries freely.

☐ Strongly Agree   ☐ Agree   ☐ Neutral   ☐ Disagree   ☐ Strongly Disagree

Explore your level of comfort with feeling vulnerable. What is making you feel more or less likely to share today?

_____

_____

_____

_____

_____

Clinician Note: Once this concept has been introduced in session, it can be used as a carryover tool to help build positive discussion guidelines at home.

How Do I Perceive Others?

. . . .

A perception is how we view a person simply based on what we know about them. It can involve a snap judgment, using very little information. Our perceptions of others might not be true, but they determine how we interact, what we say about them, and whether we trust them. We can challenge our perceptions by learning new things about the people around us. By asking questions and showing an interest in their lives, we can learn new and important information. In this activity, think about how you perceive others. Select four individuals from your home, community, or school. Write down their names, and then state how you perceive them (e.g., happy, impatient, easygoing). Finally, challenge your perceptions by learning something new. Come up with a question you could ask this person to broaden your knowledge of them.

Name	Perception: They seem to be. . .	Challenging My Perception: I am going to ask. . .
1.		
2.		
3.		
4.		

Now that you had a chance to challenge your perceptions, were you surprised by anything you learned? Do you have a different opinion of any of these individuals now?

_____

_____

_____

How Do I Want to Be Perceived?

· ·

The way other people perceive us is a result of what they see and hear. We frequently have an idea of how we want to be perceived, but our idea does not always match reality. In order to ensure you are being perceived the way you want, it is important to focus on the qualities you want to portray. In this activity, identify five qualities you want others to see in you. Write them in the clouds below. Then, reflect on your choices by thinking about why you want to be perceived that way and if you have been successful.

Reflection Questions

Why did you choose these qualities?

_____

_____

What do these qualities look like at home?

_____

_____

What do these qualities look like at school?

_____

_____

Did you demonstrate these qualities this week? Why or why not?

_____

_____

How can you demonstrate these qualities next week?

_____

_____

Empathy and Humility

In working to increase resiliency following a traumatic experience, it is essential to learn how to develop strong and supportive relationships with trusted peers and adults. These bonds provide a healing framework for continued social-emotional growth. Relationships require the ability to understand the emotions of others and to sometimes put the needs of others above our own. These abilities are encompassed by two qualities: empathy and humility.

Empathy is the ability to understand and share the feelings of others, despite never having encountered a similar situation. It is different than sympathy, which requires having a shared experience. Although children who have experienced trauma sometimes want to shield themselves from expressing emotions because it can make them feel vulnerable, being empathetic opens their hearts and minds to a variety of experiences and allows their humanity to shine. Building empathy takes practice; it takes learning to be humble.

A humble person can also be considered a modest person. They don't focus solely on their own skills and strengths, but they demonstrate an interest in those around them as well. When people are humble, they identify and acknowledge what they are good at and where they have room for growth, which empowers them to seek out support when they need it. They learn that working with others serves to build their own competence and ability to advocate. In the activities that follow, children will have an opportunity to identify their strengths and challenges, as well as how they can learn from these experiences to better relate to others.

Client Worksheet

Being Humble

· · · · · · · · · · · · · · · · · ·

Although humility is sometimes mistaken for weakness, the two concepts are not the same. Being humble simply means that you can recognize your own personal strengths and challenges, which empowers you to seek help when it is needed. What does the word "humble" mean to you? Complete the word association cloud to connect words and phrases with the concept of being humble.

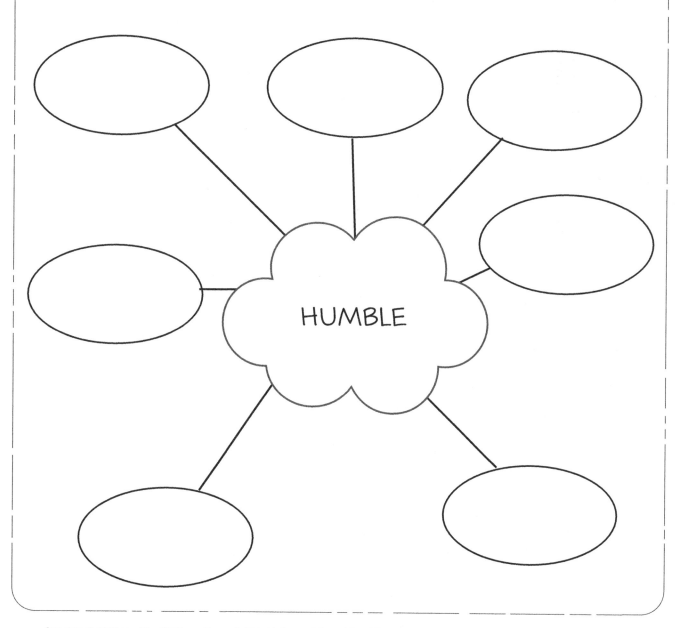

Now, think about a time when you have felt humble. What did it help you learn about yourself?

A time I felt humble was when:

_____

_____

_____

This experience helped me learn:

_____

_____

_____

Master, Apprentice, and Intern

· ·

Everyone has different strengths and challenges, as well as different levels of abilities. A master is an expert who knows almost everything about a topic. An apprentice is someone who has some skills but is still learning. An intern is just starting out and doesn't really know a lot yet. These different levels can be applied to any setting, not just school. In this activity, work with a trusted peer to determine when you are a master, an apprentice, or an intern. Use the idea bank to help guide you, but feel free to come up with your own ideas too.

Idea Bank		
Being on time	Working with others	Sharing
Communicating	Finishing my homework	Bringing my supplies
Cooking	Doing chores	Being helpful
Drawing or painting	Playing sports	Being a leader

	My View	A Friend's View
Master		
Apprentice		
Intern		

Reflection:

What can you learn from your friend?

_____

_____

Humble at Home

. . . .

Everyone cannot be good at everything. Despite what is portrayed on social media, and despite what we sometimes want to think, everyone has challenges. These challenges can occur at home, at school, or in the community. Learning to be humble allows you to recognize both your strengths and your challenges, which can help you build empathy for others. In the boxes provided, reflect on your strengths and challenges at home. You can write or draw a picture.

Something I am **great** at:

Something I am **okay** at:

Something that **challenges** me:

Now, share your thoughts with a trusted adult. Do they agree with your reflection?

❑ Agree

❑ Disagree

Humble at School

. . . .

Now that you've reflected on the strengths and challenges you have at home, take some time to reflect on how this translates to the school environment. What are your strengths and challenges at school? You can write or draw a picture.

Something I am **great** at:

Something I am **okay** at:

Something that **challenges** me:

Now, share your thoughts with a trusted adult. Do they agree with your reflection?

❑ Agree

❑ Disagree

Humble: An Empowering Reflection

· ·

Being humble means you recognize that you're not the best at everything and that you may need help or support from others at times. Learning to be humble helps you to empathize with those around you and builds self-awareness. In this activity, reflect on a time when you felt humble. What did this help you learn about yourself? For example, what emotions did you feel? What supports did you find helpful? Were there new skills you learned? What did you learn about others? How did you feel about others around you, or what were others willing to help you with?

_____

_____

_____

_____

_____

_____

_____

_____

_____

_____

_____

What I learned about myself:

_____

_____

_____

_____

What I learned about others:

_____

_____

_____

_____

CHAPTER FOUR

From Reliving to Relieving: Self-Regulation Strategies

Regulating Emotions

Emotions can be dangerous for children who have experienced trauma. Whether it stems from inconsistent responses from trusted adults or personal traumatic experiences, a variety of disruptive behaviors can emerge when children are trying to mask their inner emotions. When faced with a challenge or stressor, the child experiences an immediate fear reaction that results in displays of disrespect, disengagement, or disruption. These behaviors represent a child's ingrained survival response, which causes them to constantly be on guard. The activities in this section will help children take the first step in developing self-regulation skills. They will learn how to build their emotional vocabulary, recognize their own experiences of emotions, and identify ways to manage big emotions.

Emotions Palette

· ·

Just like painters use a palette of color to express their work, you can create an emotional palette with a variety of words that explain your different moods. Building your emotional vocabulary helps you better convey how you are feeling to others. With the help of a caregiver or trusted adult, complete the activity by creating a colorful palette of emotions or feeling words. For each circle of emotion, add other "shades" or words within that same circle that have a similar meaning. For example, other words that describe feeling sad may include gloomy, upset, and tearful. Then, fill in each circle with a color that represents how that emotion feels to you. Post your palette on your refrigerator or keep it nearby so you can refer to the list to help express yourself.

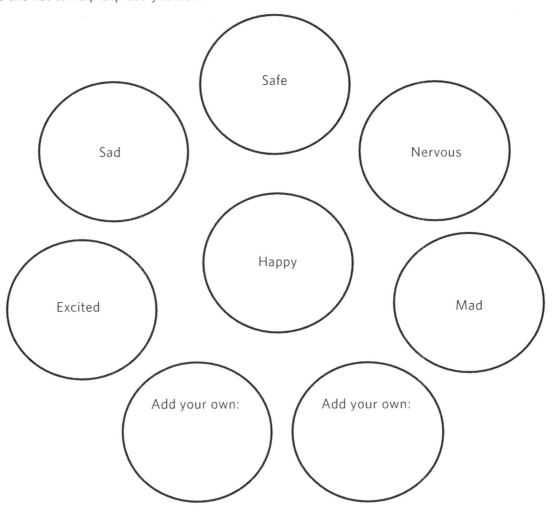

How Do You Feel?

. . . .

Situations or events can create a variety of feelings. Feelings and experiences are personal, meaning that everyone won't feel the same way in response to the same event. It is important for you to express how you feel, and you'll have a chance to practice doing so in this activity. Using the emotional palette you created in the previous activity, read each scenario and write a feeling word in the box that matches how *you* would feel. Then, shade the box with the color represented in your emotional palette.

You make a new friend:	You get invited to a party:	You are starting a new school:

Your friend or family member does not see your side of a situation:	Someone gives you a compliment:

You misplace your homework:	You get into an argument:	You fall off your bike in front of your friends:

Create your own:	Create your own:

Create your own:	Create your own:

Client and Caregiver Worksheet

Body Language
. . . .

Emotions can produce a range of responses that affect your body and mind. For example, big emotions like anger or excitement can make your heart race or cause your mind to run a million miles a minute. Other emotions, like sadness, can make your mind wander or your muscles feel sluggish. Use this activity to explore how your body responds to emotion. Think about each emotion listed here, and describe the differences felt with each one. When you are done, ask a friend or trusted adult the same questions and see if their responses are the same or different. Remember, your response is your own. There are no right or wrong answers, but it is possible to have similar feelings with others.

	Excited	Angry	Worried	Sad
How do your hands feel? Sweaty, dry, or cool?				
How do your muscles feel? Clenched, tingly, or relaxed?				
What is your mind doing? Wandering, racing, or tired?				
What is your heartbeat like? Fast, slow, or normal?				
How are you talking? Loud, fast, or slow?				
How is your breathing? Rapid, shallow, or relaxed?				
Other:				

Managing Big Emotions

· ·

In order to cope with challenges, you must be able to describe and recognize how you are feeling. What kinds of emotions do you have when you are calm compared to when you are in fight, flight, or freeze mode? The emotions are way different, right? Using the feeling words below, sort each feeling into the corresponding boxes that have been provided. Note that some emotions may fall into more than one category.

Sad	Joyful	Ashamed	Frustrated
Happy	Embarrassed	Distressed	Hopeless
Uneasy	Afraid	Panicked	Furious
Worried	Shocked	Disappointed	Cheerful
Explosive	Helpless	Surprised	

Calm

Fight

Flight

Freeze

Face Your Fear

. . . .

Sometimes, we just need a reminder that we can handle life's situations. Remember, *you can do it*! In the space provided, draw your fear face. How do your eyes or mouth look? What colors will you use? Now that you have acknowledged your fears, it's time to face them with confidence. Draw your calm, cool, and confident face. This is what your face looks like when you are in control. In the boxes that follow, write down any thoughts, feelings, and actions that might occur when you have a fear face versus a confident face. What can you do to help you move away from your fear face and show your confident face?

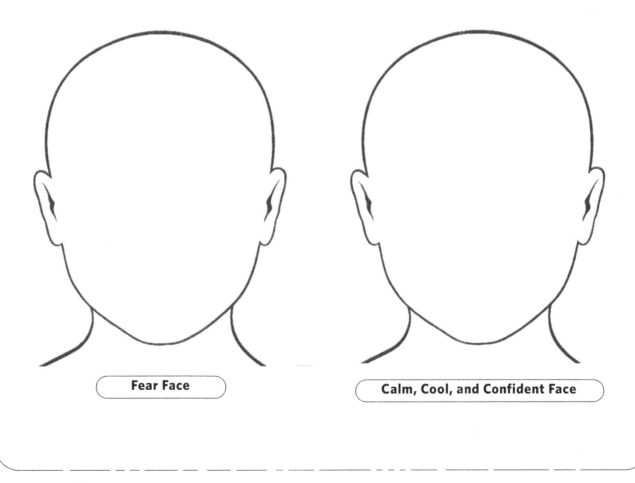

Fear Face

Calm, Cool, and Confident Face

	Fear Face	Calm, Cool, and Confident Face
Thoughts		
Feelings		
Actions		

Feelings Addition: Add It Up

. . . .

Our feelings are connected to our thoughts and actions. That is, the way we think about ourselves and the world influences the actions we take and the way we feel. If you think and act in a negative manner, it can lead to negative feelings—but if you think and act in a positive manner, it can lead to positive feelings. In the boxes below, write or illustrate a thought and action that might match the feeling answer.

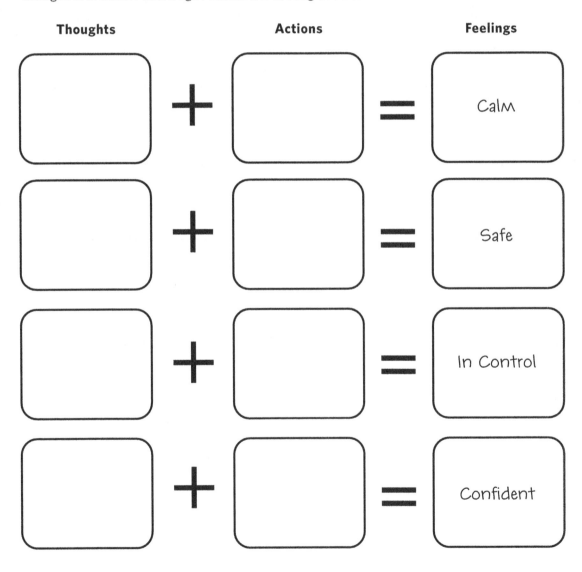

Thoughts		Actions		Feelings
	+		=	Calm
	+		=	Safe
	+		=	In Control
	+		=	Confident

Coping Skills and Supports

Coping skills are methods used to manage big emotions, reduce worry or tension, and return to a calmer state. Some coping methods are helpful and healthy, like using deep breathing or mindfulness to focus on the present moment. Other coping strategies may temporarily make things less intense—like overeating or shutting down—but these strategies are not healthy because they are a form of avoidance or distraction that actually end up creating more stress.

In this section, children will learn to differentiate between healthy versus unhealthy coping skills, and they'll have an opportunity to explore healthy skills to help them tolerate stressful situations. Since coping preferences will vary by child, this section presents a variety of activities to allow clients to find out what works best for them. Ultimately, the goal is to provide a safe space where children can build positive coping skills and reach out to trusted adults to strengthen their skills.

Exploring Coping Skills

· ·

Coping skills are the "tools" we use to help manage emotions and stay in control. When we are faced with challenging or upsetting situations, we use our coping skills to bring back feelings of safety, calmness, and control. Explore the list of coping skills provided here and see if you have used any of these skills to get through stressful times. What can you add to the coping skills list? Circle any skills you have tried, and brainstorm additional skills you might like to try.

Mindfulness	Relational
• Journaling	• Visiting with a friend
• Being creative	• Calling a friend
• Meditating	• Talking with a trusted adult
• Setting positive intentions	• Being around others
• Playing a game	• Helping others
• List your own: _____	• List your own: _____
Physical	**Sensory**
• Exercising	• Listening to music
• Stretching	• Smelling calming scents
• Deep breathing/belly breathing	• Tasting food or drink
• Muscle relaxation	• Playing with fidget toys
• Jumping (e.g., jump rope, trampoline)	• Using a weighted blanket
• List your own: _____	• Visualizing calming places
	• List your own: _____

Identify two new coping skills you would like to use and complete the statements below.

When I feel _____, I will _____ to be calm and in control.

When I feel _____, I will _____ to be calm and in control.

Calm or Crazy Coping Skills

· ·

When the going gets tough, you get coping! However, not all coping methods are helpful. Helpful coping skills, like deep breathing or journaling, allow you to manage your emotions and perform to the best of your ability. In contrast, unhelpful coping skills, like bingeing on ice cream or avoiding studying for a hard test, may provide quick relief but don't help you handle the uncomfortable situation. Therefore, it is important to have healthy coping skills in your toolbox so you can deal with uncomfortable situations or feelings and respond in a logical manner. Review the coping skills listed here, and then give an example of a calm way of using that skill versus a crazy or unhelpful way of using that skill.

Coping Skill	Calm and Helpful	Crazy or Unhelpful
Deep breathing	Example: There is a pop quiz and you use breathing methods like "breathe in the roses and blow out the candles" to calm the body so you can focus.	Example: There is a pop quiz and you panic. You start breathing loud and fast, making you light headed. You ask to go to the nurse, avoiding the task completely.
Talk with a friend		
Listen to music		
Use a fidget, toy, or sensory object		
Add your own:		

Coping and Feelings Thermometer

· ·

Feelings can range in intensity from light and manageable to heavy and out of control. A range of coping skills can be used to provide relief for these different levels of feelings. With the help of your clinician, review the list of coping skills provided here and add any other coping ideas to the list. Then, on the coping card that follows, match your favorite coping skills to each level of emotion using the feelings thermometer as a guide. Keep the card so you can use it at home or school to communicate how you're feeling and to remind you of coping strategies you can use.

Coping Ideas

- Practice deep breathing exercises (e.g., blow out the candles, balloon breathing)

- Do mindful coloring or mazes

- Tense muscles and then relax them

- Write it down on paper and throw it out

- Take a break in another area

- Speak with a trusted adult

- Play with fidgets

- Say a positive phrase like, "I am calm and cool."

- Blow bubbles

- Other: _____

- Other: _____

Coping Card	
Feeling	**Coping Skills**
I FEEL OUT OF CONTROL!	
This is making me mad!	
I feel nervous or upset.	
Something is bothering me.	
I can handle this.	

Coping and Capable

· ·

Now that you have identified healthy versus harmful coping strategies, it's time to make a positive change. Focusing on healthy strategies will ensure that you can break free of stressful situations and keep moving forward. In this activity, pick a negative emotion from the word bank that you might feel when you're stressed (or insert your own). Then, choose a positive coping strategy you can use to help move you toward a desired outcome. Finally, describe how that coping skill will help you feel more capable.

<table>
<tr><td>

Negative Emotions Word Bank

Sad, angry, irritable, tired, guilty, alone, helpless, shameful, distracted

</td><td>

Positive Coping Skills Word Bank

Take a break, listen to music, talk to a trusted adult, concentrate on breathing, use meditation, distract yourself

</td></tr>
</table>

At home:

When I feel _____

I choose to _____

To help me _____

At school:

When I feel _____

I choose to _____

To help me _____

In the community:

When I feel _____

I choose to _____

To help me _____

Design Your Own Coping Space

· ·

In the box provided, create your own personal coping space. Use your imagination and design a safe place where you can relax, recharge, and reconnect.

- Where would your space be? At home, at school, or somewhere else?

- What colors would you want to decorate the space with?

- What type of light would you like in this space (e.g., lamp, natural light)?

- What types of comfort items would you have? Think of toys, pillows, games, or anything else you might want to have in this space.

- What kind of furniture is in your space?

- What kind of music would you hear?

- Who would be there?

- What activities would you like to do in your safe space?

- What kind of scents would you want? For example, you might like the smell of your favorite candle, or the fresh air coming in through an open window.

In-Session Activity

Find Your Words

. . . .

It can be difficult to start a conversation when we are upset, angry, or stressed. In this activity, clinicians and caregivers help clients create a sensory box that they can use to regain composure, to regulate feelings, and to open communication. Ideally, this tool can be used across multiple settings.

Materials Needed:

- Small plastic bin or shoe box

- Rice or sand

- Small objects (bouncy balls, building blocks, small toys)

- Small pieces of cardstock, cardboard, or plastic

Directions:

Fill the plastic bin with rice or sand. Then, write words or draw emojis on small pieces of cardstock or on objects (small toys) and place them in the box. Have the child dig through the box to see what they find. Model how to use the box with your child or client when they are calm and not in distress. Encourage them to describe the object and how the object makes them feel. To encourage communication with older clients, write down words or sentence starters and have them describe the emotion or use statements.

Feeling Ideas

Happy	Irritated	Peaceful
Relaxed	Angry	Tired
Sad	Distracted	Worried

Statement Ideas

Name a person you trust.

Take three deep breaths.

What was the last moment that made you laugh?

Cool and Calm Reminder

· ·

What activities help you keep calm and cool when your stress or frustration level reaches maximum capacity? Since we don't always make the best decisions when we are really upset, brainstorm positive solutions to help you maintain your cool ahead of time. Create a cool and calm reminder logo that will remind you what it looks and feels like to use these coping strategies.

What strategies help you maintain your cool?

- Talk to a trusted person
- Take some time to myself
- Have a snack or water break
- Take a movement break (e.g., walk, jump, stretch)

- _____
- _____
- _____
- _____

My Cool and Calm Reminder Logo

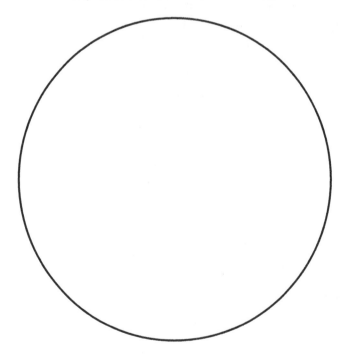

Bad Day Do-Over

. . . .

Sometimes, we have bad days. These difficult times can be caused by a variety of reasons, but it's important not to get stuck in a cycle of negative experiences. In order to move forward, you need to learn how to break free of bad days. In this activity, reflect on what a bad day looks like for you. Then, think about what supports you need from a trusted friend or adult, as well as which coping skills you can use, to break free of your bad day.

When I have a bad day, it looks like:

Actions: _____

_____

_____

Emotions and body sensations: _____

_____

_____

Thoughts: _____

_____

_____

Other: _____

_____

_____

To re-do my bad day, I need:

Coping skills: _____

_____

_____

Places I can go: _____

_____

_____

Trusted friends or adults who can help: _____

_____

_____

Other: _____

_____

Client Worksheet

Helping Hands

· · · · · · · · · · · · · · · · · · · ·

Everyone has days when they struggle. It is important to know that there are people around you who you can reach out to for support and that you are not alone. In this activity, reflect on who you reach out to for help, as well as who has reached out to you.

Who do you go to for help?

At home	
At school	
In the community	

Who has asked you for help?

At home	
At school	
In the community	

Reflection:

How does it make you feel to know you can help others?

Happy

Okay

Not Happy

I Am Connected

. . . .

When faced with a stressful situation or overwhelming feelings, it is easy to forget that there are others who can help us. Create a card as a reminder that you are connected and that there are trusted adults who can help you. Complete the card provided, decorate it, and cut it out. Whenever you need a reminder, read the card, recite the positive intention, and know that you are supported.

Example: If I am feeling (insert feeling) **overwhelmed**, I can reach out to (support person) ***a trusted adult or friend*** for support.

Positive Thought Reminder:

I am loved. I am connected.

I Am Connected

If I am feeling _____,

I can reach out to _____ for support.

Positive Thought Reminder:

_____

_____

_____

On-the-Go Calming Kit

• •

Create a calming kit to use on the go. In a small bin, collect a few items to create a calming kit you can use when you are traveling between places, houses, or some other location.

- Ideas to promote mindful breathing: pinwheels, bubbles
- Ideas to calm the mind: coloring materials, favorite books, puzzles
- Ideas to calm the body: fidget toys, rubber bands, stress balls, favorite scents
- Ideas to communicate your emotions: emoji symbols, a feelings thermometer

My Kit:

-
-
-
-
-
-
-
-
-
-

Mindful Practice

Mindfulness activities provide an opportunity to take a step back, connect with the present, and let go of distractions around us. These techniques help us check our bodies and minds so we can find a moment of calm in the whirlwind of life. In this section, children will find mindfulness activities they can use to connect with their body, mind, and senses. By taking notice of small details in their surroundings or learning to control their breathing, they can learn to find a calm mindset. In this section, a variety of mindfulness activities are provided so children can explore which breathing, grounding, and gratitude techniques work best for them. These activities can be combined to create a routine to destress and relax even when times are tough.

Wave Breathing

. . . .

Controlling your breathing is an effective way to maintain your cool and to disconnect from things that may be bothering you. Read the breathing script aloud or have your caregiver read it to you. Follow the design of the wave as you listen to the script, focusing on your body and stillness during this exercise. You can also try adding texture or color to the wave by coloring it.

Breathing Script

Breathe in as you ride up the wave. Counting slowly... 1, 2, 3. Pause at the crest of the wave, balancing your body on the water, counting 4, 5, 6. Breathe out as you follow the wave back down to the water line, counting 7, 8, 9, 10.

Mindful Mountain

· ·

Letting go isn't always easy. It can feel like you are climbing up a mountain carrying your stress, worry, or fear. In order to let go, you must acknowledge your thoughts and challenges, as well as validate your feelings, along the way. You can use this activity whenever you are struggling with stress or frustration. As uncomfortable feelings start to creep up, address these feelings and then let it all go using this breathing script.

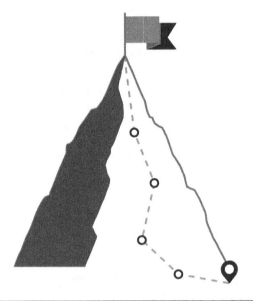

Mountain Script

As you climb up the mountain, take a deep breath in as you count to 10. Hold your breath at the top of the peak, acknowledging your challenges and efforts. Breathe out as you remind yourself that you are in control.

Grounding Scripts

. . . .

Grounding techniques are simple, quick activities to help you connect with the present moment by focusing on your surroundings and disconnecting from challenging thoughts or feelings. This type of activity can be used to help you when you start to feel uncomfortable or worried. Using the Safety Grounding Script as an example, create your own grounding script with things that make you feel safe and calm.

Safety Grounding Script

5.   Name 5 people you trust.

4.   Name 4 places that are safe.

3.   Name 3 comfortable feelings.

2.   Name 2 coping skills to help you feel safer.

1.   Say 1 positive saying like, "I can do this!" or "I am loved."

Personal Grounding Script

5.   _____

4.   _____

3.   _____

2.   _____

1.   _____

Client Activity

Mandala Coloring

· ·

Mandalas are circular geometric designs with repeating patterns. Coloring a mandala requires patience and focus, which are both elements of mindfulness. The act of concentrating while coloring will help you relax, let go of stress, and focus on the present. Use colored pencils, fine tip markers, or gel pens to create a beautiful design. Let your creativity fly by using a variety of colors to complete your mandala.

Mindful Mandala

. . . .

Create your own mandala using the template provided. Make a unique design that goes around each ring by using a variety of shapes, marks, and patterns to make your design truly yours. Make your mandala stand out by using a wide range of colors.

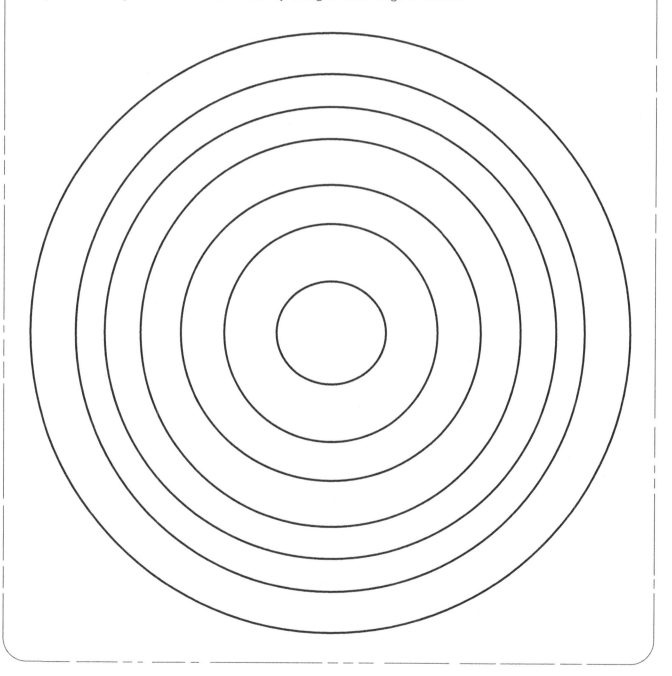

Client and Caregiver Worksheet

Love Language

. . . .

Love language is unique to each person because there are so many ways to feel love and show love. Caregivers and children show love in a variety of ways. For instance, a child might feel loved by getting a hug or playing a game with a family member, whereas a caregiver might feel love whenever someone asks how they are feeling or when they spend time with loved ones. Being mindful of differences in how we give and feel love can help increase connection with others. Caregivers and children can follow the outline of the heart and take turns listing ways they feel or show love. In the middle heart, they can list the common elements of their family love language.

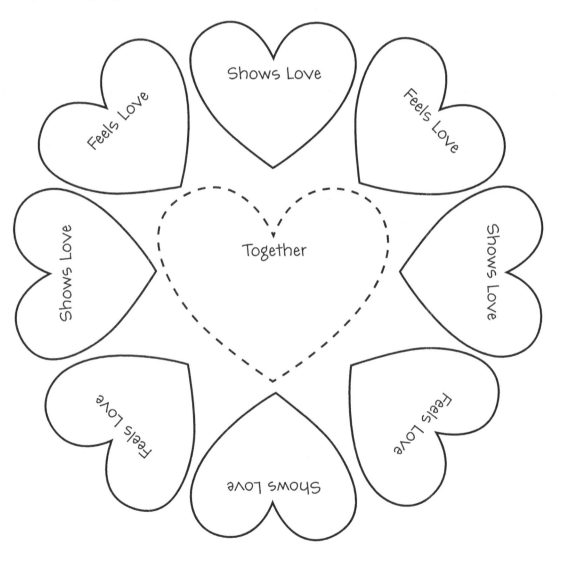

Client Worksheet

Daily DJ

· · · · · · · · · · ·

Music is a great way to prime the body and mind for challenging tasks. The right beat can get the heart pumping and the good vibes flowing, which helps you get ready to take on the day. Likewise, softer tones or slower beats can help you to calm your body and mind, rebound from a frustrating moment, or chill out. What music speaks to you? Unleash your inner DJ and create "warm-up" and "chill-out" playlists below.

Top 5 Warm-Up Songs

Times this list will be helpful: _____

1. _____

2. _____

3. _____

4. _____

5. _____

Top 5 Chill-Out Songs

Times this list will be helpful: _____

1. _____

2. _____

3. _____

4. _____

5. _____

Mindful Mealtime

. . . .

Exploring food is a fun way to connect to the present and use our senses to describe something that is part of our daily life. Using all five of your senses, take a moment and describe your meal, whether it be your after-school snack or family dinner. Note as many colors, smells, flavors, textures, and sounds as you can. Work together with other family members to describe as many details of the meal.

Challenge: Take this activity one step further and make your most mindful meal with your caregiver. Consider your preferences for taste, smell, texture, and color. Then share your mindful creation with your family!

Menu: _____

Sight: _____

Smell: _____

Taste: _____

Touch: _____

Sound: _____

I Spy with My Five Senses

· ·

Game time! I spy is a guessing game where you pick an object and describe what it looks like without naming what it is. This time, change it up by describing objects with all your senses. First, find a partner, friend, or family member who can play along with you. Then, take turns selecting an object to describe. Without saying what the object is, use your senses to describe the item. See if the other player can guess what the object is!

I spy with my mind...

Smells like: _____

Feels like: _____

Sounds like: _____

Tastes like: _____

Looks like: _____

Mindful Minute

• •

Take a minute (or three) to play a mindful minute game! These are a great way to help make talking about emotions, coping skills, and healthy habits easier. The directions are simple: Set a timer for one minute, read the task, and create as many answers as you can. You can list your answers in the boxes below or have a partner write for you. Try repeating this task again in a few weeks to see your growth! You can also make this into a game by challenging a friend or family member to see how many answers they can come up. Who can create a longer list?

Task 1: List as many emotions as you can in 60 seconds. Go!

Task 2: List as many coping skills as you can in 60 seconds. Go!

Task 3: List as many healthy habits as you can in 60 seconds. Go!

Track your progress! Record how many answers you are able to come up with each time.

	Date:	Date:	Date:
Number of Emotions			
Number of Coping Skills			
Number of Healthy Habits			

CHAPTER FIVE

Thawing the Freeze: Building Problem-Solving Pathways

Mindset Manager

There is more than one way to solve a problem, but not all paths lead to positive or helpful solutions. Effective problem solving requires that we practice being patient, review all possible choices, and make the best decision based on the information we have. One's ability to problem solve tends to freeze when the pressure is on. High levels of stress and poor decision-making skills can cause people to react emotionally rather than take a step back and analyze the situation. Having a calm and relaxed mindset allows children to brainstorm different solutions, examine the consequences of each (the good and the bad!), and make the best decision for the situation. The activities ahead bring awareness to different problem-solving mindsets and give scenarios to practice decision-making skills.

Problem-Solving Mindset

· ·

Are you ready to problem solve? Our bodies must be calm and cool in order to make the best decisions. When we're upset, our minds become reactive, which limits our ability to think about what might happen or the consequences of our actions. When we are sad or reluctant, our problem-solving abilities also decrease, often leading us to avoid or escape a problem. Review the mindsets here and reflect on a time you used each of the mindsets.

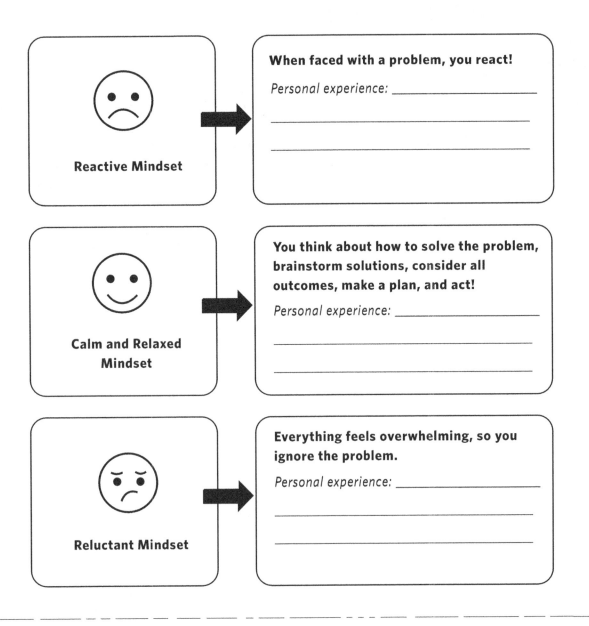

Reactive Mindset

When faced with a problem, you react!

Personal experience: _____

_____

_____

Calm and Relaxed Mindset

You think about how to solve the problem, brainstorm solutions, consider all outcomes, make a plan, and act!

Personal experience: _____

_____

_____

Reluctant Mindset

Everything feels overwhelming, so you ignore the problem.

Personal experience: _____

_____

_____

Mindset Reminders

. . . .

Step 1: Create an icon that represents each of the problem-solving mindsets: reactive, relaxed, and reluctant. Use colors, symbols, or images to make your icon stand out.

Reactive!	**Relaxed.**	**Reluctant...**

Step 2: Sort the examples provided, or use your own examples, and place them in the corresponding mindset boxes below.

Examples:

Yelling at someone	Telling a friend when they hurt your feelings
Walking away from a fight	Putting your head down when frustrated
Hiding in the bathroom	Not yelling when someone says something unkind
Asking for help	Stomping your feet when you don't get your way

Reactive	Relaxed	Reluctant

Mindset Jar

· · · · · · · · · · · · · · · ·

What do you do when you feel frozen? When you're faced with a problem but are unable to get going? Sometimes, it is helpful to take a break, distract yourself for a few minutes, and then come back and attempt to solve the problem again. Review the ideas here and add a few of your own. Then, cut the cards out and place them in a mindset jar (or a can, envelope, or whatever you have!). Next time you get stuck, reach into your "jar," perform the quick task, and then get back to problem solving.

Tell a joke to a friend. For example: "Why did the teddy bear say no to dessert?" *Because he was stuffed.*	Find a place away from your work area, preferably somewhere sunny. Practice a few rounds of deep breathing. Breathe in and smell the roses, breathe out and blow out the candles.	Take a brief break from your problem. Complete one other thing on your to-do list. For example: clean up, do a chore, or walk the dog.
Think about the last time you solved a challenging issue. List two positive strategies that helped you solve the problem.	Take a short walk outside, and take a deep breath in. What do you smell? Look around and name three things you see.	Stand up and do five yoga moves. Some ideas include downward dog, child's pose, tree pose, and cat/cow.
Make a snack, eat it in another room, and then come back and tackle your problem.	Say a positive saying to yourself three times. For example: "I can handle this. I'm a problem solver."	Tell a joke to a friend. For example: "What did one plate say to the other plate?" *Dinner is on me!*
Create your own:	Create your own:	Create your own:

Problems and Options: Part 1

· ·

As you've learned, the type of mindset you are in (reactive, relaxed, or reluctant) has a big influence over how you respond to a given situation. Review the scenarios listed here and brainstorm different ways to react. Then, provide your own scenario and list options for reacting.

Scenario 1: Cal failed a math test yesterday but was able to make corrections in order to boost his grade. However, when he got home, he was not able find his test in his cluttered backpack and started to panic.

☹ Reactive Option:

_____

_____

☺ Relaxed Option:

_____

_____

😠 Reluctant Option:

_____

_____

Scenario 2: Jordan was sweeping up a mess in the kitchen after spilling cereal on the floor. Suddenly the pile of cereal got scattered around the room again after her sister chased the dog through the kitchen.

🙁 Reactive Option:

_____

_____

🙂 Relaxed Option:

_____

_____

😠 Reluctant Option:

_____

_____

Create your own scenario: _____

_____

🙁 Reactive Option:

_____

_____

🙂 Relaxed Option:

_____

_____

😠 Reluctant Option:

_____

_____

Problems and Consequences: Part 2

· ·

With every decision comes a consequence. Eek! Perhaps the word "consequence" sounds scary to you, but keep in mind that it is just another name for the result of an action, whether it is good, bad, or somewhere in the middle. Choose a scenario and list the different consequences for each of the mindsets. An example is provided for you first.

Scenario: A friend embarrasses you at the playground.

Reactive option: You yell at your friend.

Consequence: You continue to feel upset, and now your friend is also upset.

Reluctant option: You hide behind a bush so no one sees you.

Consequence: Your friend doesn't know that they hurt your feelings. You miss out on playing with others.

Relaxed option: You take a deep breath and tell your friend, "I felt embarrassed because you made fun of me."

Consequence: You expressed your feelings in a positive manner. You're possibly able to move on with your friend, and you don't get into trouble.

Scenario:

_____

_____

_____

😦 **Reactive option:** _____

    Consequences: _____

_____

_____

😠 **Reluctant option:** _____

    Consequences: _____

_____

_____

😊 **Relaxed option:** _____

    Consequences: _____

_____

_____

Decision Making

The activities in this section help clients practice solving scenarios in a low-risk environment. Practicing decision-making skills can help prepare clients for real-life scenarios when the pressure is on. When children are in control of their thoughts and emotions, they can view events with reason and logic, which helps them take the best course of action. This reasoning allows them to better predict consequences, ensuring that they make the best decisions for themselves and for their personal growth.

Client Worksheet

Marvelous Mindset

· ·

Meet *Marvelous*, your own inner hero with superpowers enabling you to melt the problem-solving freeze! Create Marvelous' profile below by listing out their additional superpowers, picking a superhero sidekick, and adding other fun details. Then, create an image of your new inner superhero.

Profile

Wears a Mask? Yes or No

Wears a Cape? Yes or No

Daytime Job: _____

Favorite Color: _____

Superpowers:

- Able to melt the problem-solving freeze!

-

-

-

-

Draw Your Superhero:

Trusted Sidekick:

Name:

Description:

How does your trusted sidekick help you feel calm and in control when faced with tough problems? (e.g., play your "super song" to get you amped up)

Client Worksheet

Marvelous Mindset in Action

· · · · · · · · · · · ·

You and your trusted sidekick just enrolled in Superhero Academy and are getting ready for your first meeting: problem-solving skills. You're new at being a hero and are feeling a bit jittery, but with your abilities, you are confident that you can do it! To get prepared, you decide to do a bit of problem-solving practice before heading out. In this activity, review the scenarios given and select one to problem solve. Identify what the potential problems are, what fears people have, and then determine the best solution.

Step 1: Select a Scenario

Scenario A: Darius and Danielle are arguing about whether to tell their caregiver about a broken toy. What advice can you give the siblings?

Scenario B: While playing basketball at recess, Sean bumped into Tommy, and he lost the ball. Tommy disrupts the game by yelling at Sean. What advice can you give Tommy?

Scenario C: Create your own scenario: _____

_____

_____

Step 2: Using the scenario you selected in Step 1, answer the following questions:

Identify the problem			
What are the feelings involved?			
Name one positive action they could take.		Describe the possible outcome.	
Name one negative action they could take.		Describe the possible outcome.	

Step 3: Now that you have had some practice problem solving, are you more confident putting problem-solving skills in action? Why or why not?

_____

_____

Problem-Solving Scenarios

· ·

In this activity, you'll read through each of the following four scenarios and select the problem-solving mindset that matches the situation. At the end of the activity, you'll find the answers, but try not to peek until you are finished!

Scenario 1: Leah was at a birthday party with several friends. Two of the girls laughed at Leah when she dropped a cupcake on the floor. Initially embarrassed, Leah ran to the bathroom. She took a few deep breaths and got cleaned up. Her feelings were hurt, and as she wiped away her tears, she decided to tell the girls how they made her feel.

What was Leah's problem-solving mindset?

     A. Reactive

     B. Relaxed

     C. Reluctant

Scenario 2: At recess, Jonathon was playing a game with his friends. Jonathon lost and became upset. He yelled out, "That is not how you play the game! No one is listening to me. I don't want to play anymore!" He threw the ball and walked away.

What was Jonathon's problem-solving mindset?

     A. Reactive

     B. Relaxed

     C. Reluctant

Scenario 3: Cody heard his parents arguing about money in the living room. He was supposed to be doing homework in his room, but his parents' voices were too loud for him to concentrate. Upset, Cody headed to his room. He put on music for a while and ignored his mother when she called out that it was dinner time. After Cody cooled off, he decided to tell his mom that he was upset. Cody told his mom that he was sad when he heard his parents arguing.

What was Cody's problem-solving mindset?

      A. Reactive

      B. Relaxed

      C. Reluctant

Scenario 4: Ana had to take an unexpected mathematics test at school. To the teachers, the test just involved assessing what the class already knew. But as Ana started the test, she became less focused and started to panic. She did not understand the directions, which caused her to quickly become upset. She put her head down and refused to take the test.

What was Ana's problem-solving mindset?

      A. Reactive

      B. Relaxed

      C. Reluctant

1. B, 2. A, 3. B, 4. C

Problem-Responding Worksheet

· ·

Are you ready? When you are calm and ready, write down a current problem you are experiencing. With a trusted partner, list three different options for responding to your problem. Consider the consequences (results) of each option and select your best choice, or revise an option to make a decision.

Current Problem:

_____

_____

_____

Option 1: _____

_____

_____

Option 2: _____

_____

_____

Option 3: _____

_____

_____

Thoughts to ponder...

- Have you solved this type of problem before? If so, what worked?

- Have you seen someone else solve this type of problem before? If yes, what worked?

- Is there someone who can help you? If so, who?

What is the best option for my situation?

I will solve my problem by _____

_____

_____

_____

_____

This will help me feel _____

_____

_____

_____

_____

Calm and Relaxed Think Sheet

· ·

Calm and cool is the best way to face a challenging situation. Use this think sheet as a guide to help you through the decision-making process. Identify a personal problem or challenge. Brainstorm different ways to solve it, while also looking at the various outcomes, and then select the best choice for your situation.

1. Identify the Problem:	
2. Possible Solution A:	Possible Consequences:
3. Possible Solution B:	Possible Consequences:
4. Possible Solution C:	Possible Consequences:

My best solution is _____

My plan is _____

_____

If I need help, I can ask _____

I am a calm and relaxed problem solver.

Coping with Change

Everyone can attest to the following statement: **Change is Hard**. It means dealing with the unfamiliar, the unexpected, and the unknown. People find comfort in patterns, familiarity, and consistency, so when something is new or different, it comes as a physical shock to the system. While it may seem that avoiding change may be a way to maintain a safe environment, especially for children who have experienced trauma, the reality is that this can prevent personal progress. Therefore, the activities that follow will help children break out of the familiar so they can reach their full potential.

The first step on the journey to change is helping children recognize that there is something they want to be different. It might sound like this is easy or obvious, but this recognition actually shows that they are ready for growth. Being able to identify that a change is needed shows that children are reflecting on their decisions or actions and that they can see there may be a better way to handle events. This recognition leads them to explore alternatives and to make a commitment to try something different. Exploring something new does not always have to be on a large scale. Small changes can also have a large impact on a child's day-to-day life. The important aspect is being open to the possibility of change in order to promote flexible, dynamic thinking, and encourage personal empowerment.

Client Worksheet

Making a Back-Up Plan

· ·

Change happens! When change catches us off guard, it can make us feel unsafe or frustrated, and that can impact our ability to problem solve. Take this opportunity to reflect on a time when you had to handle a change in your daily routine. Acknowledge how you felt and any coping skills that helped you handle the change. Then, brainstorm another back-up plan to help you feel safe the next time you are faced with an unexpected change.

Step 1: Describe your typical routine and what changed:

What normally happens?	**What changed?**

Step 2: Describe how this made you feel:

Happy   Worried   Anxious   Unsure

Upset   Frustrated   Angry   Other: _____

Step 3: Circle any coping skills you were able to use to feel better:

Asking for help   Talking to a trusted adult   Deep breathing   Drawing

Listening to music   Taking a short break   Sitting quietly   Other: _____

Step 4: Make a back-up plan! If this happens again, what are three positive actions you can take to handle the change?

1. _____

2. _____

3. _____

One Foot Forward

. . . .

The idea of making a change can be overwhelming. Once you have committed to change and moved away from self-doubt, you must decide how to get started. Big changes don't happen overnight so you need to start small! Even the smallest shift can have a big difference down the road. Monitoring your small changes can show you how far you have come. In this activity, you are going to chart your progress. First, write down your goal. Then, every time you make a small change to achieve that goal, write it out, and color in a footstep on your pathway.

Example: Arriving to school on time.

Small Step 1: Pick out my outfit the night before.

Small Step 2: Pack my backpack the night before.

Small Step 3: Set my alarm five minutes earlier to give me more time to wake up.

My goal: _____

Small Step 1: _____

_____

Small Step 2: _____

_____

Small Step 3: _____

_____

Eek! I'm Trying Something New and Different

· ·

Being afraid of new things can sometimes prevent us from exploring new and different possibilities. It's important to confront those fears head-on so you can continue to grow and change. In this activity, you will think of a time you had to try something new and different. What fears did you have? What were some of your other feelings? Afterward, what were the good and bad outcomes?

A time I tried something new or different:

_____

_____

_____

My Thoughts:	My Feelings:
_____	_____
_____	_____

Good Outcomes:	Bad Outcomes:
_____	_____
_____	_____
_____	_____

What would I do differently?

_____

Trying Something New

· ·

It's time to learn about a time when a trusted friend or adult tried a new experience! We tend to believe that everyone experiences things in a similar way as us, when this is not the case. Pick a trusted friend or adult to interview about a time they tried something new. Ask about their fears, feelings, and good and bad outcomes. List any ideas you can try in the future to tackle new and different experiences.

Interview Questions

1. Tell me about a time you tried something new and different:

   _____

   _____

2. What were your worries?

   _____

   _____

3. What other feelings did you have?

   _____

   _____

4. How did you keep your worries in check?

   _____

   _____

5. What were the positive outcomes, expected or unexpected, for trying something new?

   _____

   _____

6. Were there any bad or undesired outcomes?

_____

_____

Follow-up questions for you to complete after the interview:

1. How was this person's experience similar to yours?

_____

_____

_____

2. How was this person's experience different from yours?

_____

_____

_____

3. List any new ideas for managing your worries when tackling something new.

_____

_____

_____

Making a Change

. . . .

Change is hard. It's even more difficult when you continue to doubt whether that change is necessary. Frequently, change starts with a recognition that something is not quite right, but it can take a while to fully determine what needs to shift. In this activity, you are going to reflect on a specific challenge and affirm that a change needs to be made. Then, you will reflect on what is not working and what needs to change.

My Challenge Area Is:

☐ I recognize that I need to make a change in order to improve my well-being.

_____

(Signature)

What's not working?

- _____
- _____
- _____
- _____

What needs to change?

- _____
- _____
- _____
- _____

Now, what doubts do you have? Reflect on whether these doubts are legitimate (**fact**) or just excuses (**fiction**).

Doubts:

Fact or Fiction?

- _____

- _____

- _____

- _____

- _____

- _____

- _____

- _____

Owning Our Choices

· ·

Every day, we must make a lot of different choices. Some are small, and some are large. It's common for us to start doubting our choices by second-guessing them. But that self-doubt can be crippling, and it can prevent us from moving forward. In this activity, you'll practice how to own your choices. First, describe a choice you recently made. Then, express what you are worried about. Based on this information, identify your worst-case scenario, and reflect on what you can do to prevent this.

1. A choice I made:

_____

_____

_____

2. I am worried about:

_____

_____

_____

3. Worst-case scenario:

_____

_____

_____

4. I can prevent the worst-case scenario by:

Using my skills: _____

_____

Leaning on people who can support me: _____

_____

Repeating a positive mantra (or saying) to help me stay confident in my choices:

_____

CHAPTER SIX

Fostering Empowerment and Self-Care

Discovering My Inner Self

Throughout this workbook, children have been building strategies and skills in order to effectively manage emotions, problem solve, cope with changes, and build trust and understanding. At this point, they should have learned many new abilities, so it is now time to help them reflect on how their experience is unique to them and how they can develop greater self-awareness. Although it can be easy for children to look at others and make comparisons to their own lives, this can be counterproductive and may cause them to judge themselves more harshly. The activities that follow are intended to help children more realistically regard their lives and experiences, using a productive mindset that stimulates resiliency and increases adaptability. Helping children reflect on their choices, goals, and behaviors will serve to increase self-awareness and will become the building blocks of personal empowerment.

Client Worksheet

Who Am I?

. . . .

Learning about yourself, or having self-awareness, is an important part of your journey to becoming more mindful, independent, and in control. Having self-awareness allows you to mindfully reflect on your thoughts and actions without being judgmental. Let's get started. In this activity, reflect on the person you are currently, as well as the person you see yourself becoming in the future.

Name:

_____

Age:

_____

Hidden talent:

_____

The subject in school I am best at:

_____

The subject in school that challenges me the most:

_____

I could win a gold medal in:

_____

In 10 years, I see myself:

_____

In 20 years, I see myself:

_____

Share your thoughts with a trusted adult or friend. What was their reaction?

_____

_____

My Highlight Reel

· ·

A "highlight reel" involves looking at the highlights, or the most significant moments, for a given time period. Highlights are occasions that are particularly notable or important for a person. With social media, it is easy to see our friends' and family members' highlight reels, which frames our opinions about their lives. In this activity, you are going to create your own highlight reel for the past week. Then, reflect on why you would want to share that information with others. You can either write down what happened or draw a picture.

My highlights	Why would I want to share these highlights?

Reflection:

Do we tend to share more positive or negative events in our highlight reel?

_____

_____

_____

_____

Real Reel vs. Highlight Reel

When we talk to friends or acquaintances, they may only share their highlight reel. That is, the cool or important things happening in their lives. But we can't compare real-life experiences to only highlights. That creates a skewed perspective that everyone else's lives are better than ours, and it can make us think that we're the only ones who make mistakes. The reality is that everyone has a "real reel" and a "highlight reel." In this activity, you are going to create your real reel. Be honest and share four events that happened this week, whether they were positive or negative. Then, reflect on how these events helped you grow as a person. Feel free to write down your actions or draw a picture.

What happened this week?	How did it help you grow? For example, did you try something new or make a friend?

Share your experiences with a trusted adult or peer. Have they had similar experiences?

_____

_____

In-Session Activity

Self-Awareness: What's Important?

It's easy to get caught up in trivial or unimportant matters. We can become consumed by little things that don't have a big impact on our lives. These small distractions can stop us from successfully achieving our goals. It's important to keep focused on what really matters. With the help of a clinician or trusted adult, reflect on what is important in your life versus what doesn't matter and is simply a distraction.

What's important to me?	Why?
1. _____	1. _____
2. _____	2. _____
3. _____	3. _____

What's NOT important to me?	Why?
1. _____	1. _____
2. _____	2. _____
3. _____	3. _____

Based on what you found important, find a quote or create a personal motto, and write it here:

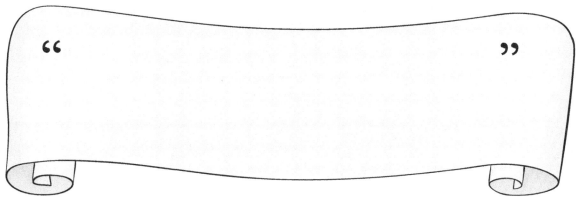

Self-Acceptance: I Love ME!

. . . .

Part of feeling empowered is having a strong sense of self-acceptance, which means that you love yourself *just as you are*. Everyone has strengths and challenges, but despite our flaws, we need to show ourselves some self-love. Being self-aware and accepting yourself allows for personal growth and empowerment. In this activity, identify all the ways that you ROCK!

Top 10 things I love about ME:

1. _____
2. _____
3. _____
4. _____
5. _____
6. _____
7. _____
8. _____
9. _____
10. _____

Now, check in with a trusted adult or peer. Come up with a few more reasons why you ROCK!

- _____
- _____
- _____
- _____

Empowerment

Self-reflection is a necessary step on the path to empowerment. In the previous section, children learned how to build self-awareness in order to focus on personal growth and resiliency. Now, it is time for them to learn how to express themselves effectively when advocating for their goals, needs, and expectations. When children are able to communicate clearly, it shows that they are confident in their knowledge and that they have expectations for those they are interacting with.

Effective communication not only involves the words that we use, but *how* we say them as well. It also involves considering the impression we want to give and the perception of those around us. Therefore, the activities in this section will help children reflect on the most effective communication methods, as well as their own personal interaction style. These tools will help children speak confidently and will allow them to share their goals and strategies with trusted peers and adults who can support them along their journey. Having the confidence to share this information demonstrates that children are empowered, no longer hiding their emotions, and no longer afraid to make changes.

Just Right Communication: Take 1: Too Much vs. Just Right

· ·

There are many types of communication styles that we use to convey information to people. An *aggressive communicator* only expresses their own wants and needs without consideration for anyone else. Their style is "too much." An *assertive communicator* can express positive and negative ideas in an open and direct way. This ensures that communication is productive and effective and that people feel respected. Their style is "just right." In this activity, review the sample scenario and consider the response of an assertive communicator versus an aggressive communicator. What do you think the outcomes would be?

Scenario: Your caregiver promised that you would be able to go out to your favorite restaurant tonight, but they just told you that it wouldn't be possible. They say they are sorry, but you are really frustrated.

"Just Right" Response (Assertive)	"Too Much" Response (Aggressive)
Example: "I'm really disappointed, but maybe we can go out another night?"	Example: "That's not fair! You always change plans!"
"Just Right" Outcome	**"Too Much" Outcome**

Reflection:

What did you notice about the "just right" outcome versus the "too much" outcome? Which one gave you what you wanted?

_____

_____

Just Right Communication: Take 2: Too Little vs. Just Right

· ·

There are many types of communication styles that we use to convey information to people. A *passive communicator* avoids sharing their feelings, wants, and needs. They do not typically respond to overtly hurtful or upsetting situations. Their style does "too little." An *assertive communicator* can express positive and negative ideas in an open and direct way. This ensures that communication is productive and effective and that people feel respected. Their style is "just right." In this activity, review the sample scenario and consider the response of an assertive communicator versus a passive communicator. What do you think the outcomes would be?

Scenario: During lunch, a peer says something negative about the new pair of shoes you got. You really like these shoes, and it is bothering you that someone would insult them.

"Just Right" Response	"Too Little" Response
Example: "It hurts my feelings that you would insult my shoes. I like them a lot."	Example: Shrugs, looks away, and doesn't say anything.
"Just Right" Outcome	**"Too Little" Outcome**

Reflection:

What did you notice about the "just right" outcome versus the "too little" outcome? Which one gave you what you wanted?

_____

_____

What Type of Communicator Am I?

• •

As you have learned, there are different ways that we can communicate our wants and needs to those around us. Not all communication methods are created equal, and certain methods are more effective than others in ensuring that a conversation is productive. This activity will allow you to reflect on your own communication style. Check the boxes that most resemble your behaviors when you interact with others. It may be beneficial for you to work with a trusted peer or adult to get their feedback as well.

"Too Little" Passive Communication	"Just Right" Assertive Communication	"Too Much" Aggressive Communication
☐ I hide or avoid feelings.	☐ I recognize and acknowledge my own feelings.	☐ I can be rude or abrupt sometimes.
☐ I fear rejection.		☐ I don't take the perspective of others.
☐ I'm afraid of disapproval.	☐ I recognize and acknowledge the feelings of others.	☐ I can be judgmental toward others.
☐ I keep my feelings inside.	☐ I can describe myself as sensitive and caring.	☐ If I feel threatened, I can be disrespectful toward others.
☐ I don't want to look "stupid" or as if I don't know what is going on.	☐ I use "I" statements a lot in discussions or arguments.	☐ I only think about what I want in a conversation.
☐ I don't like being wrong.	☐ I am tactful in discussions and do not raise my voice.	☐ I need to be right and to make a point.
☐ I can be immature.		
☐ I can feel isolated or anxious.	☐ I establish clear boundaries and expectations with peers.	☐ I use "you" a lot when arguing with others.
☐ I don't always speak up for myself.		☐ I never let anything go.

Draw a picture or write a few words that best represent your "just right" communication style:

Making an Impression

. . . .

The way we express ourselves involves more than just the words we say. It also involves the impression we give through our body language and our tone of voice. Even if what we are saying is true and important, the message can be lost if we don't approach a situation in an appropriate way. What you say is just as important as *how* you say it. In this activity, you are going to think about the best way to present information in each situation. You can also come up with your own scenarios at the end of the worksheet. Think about the words you will say, your volume and tone of voice, and how your body will look.

Scenario	How do you feel?	What will you say?	Tone and Volume	Body Presentation
You want to go to a midnight movie, but your caregiver says that it's too late.	Angry, frustrated, mistrustful	"I feel frustrated and believe that I should be allowed to go. Can you explain why you don't want to let me go?"	Even tone, normal speaking volume	Relax hands, make good eye contact, stand up straight
There is an emergency at home, and you need to share the information with your teacher.	Scared, nervous, upset			
You got a bad grade on a test, and you know you can do a better job.				

Your teacher tells you that you didn't turn in a homework assignment, but you know you did.				
Choose your own:				

Bonus: Take or draw a picture of yourself using your best body presentation, with great eye contact, relaxed hands, and straight posture. This can help to remind you how to make a good impression.

All About Me

. . . .

Self-awareness is an essential component to feeling empowered to express yourself. Not only do you need to know your personal strengths and challenges, but it is important to feel confident in sharing your accomplishments and goals with trusted peers and adults. Use this worksheet as a guide to create your own presentation about a topic you know best: YOU! Select an audience for your presentation, and then use the prompts in each box to come up with information that might be important to include in your presentation.

Select your audience: Family   Close friends   School friends   Relatives   Other: _____

I am good at...	My hidden talent is...	I would like to get better at...
I learn best by...	I am bothered by...	My favorite hobbies are...
I like to share my accomplishments with...	When I need help, I ask...	Add your own idea here!

Taking Care of Myself and Others

Life can be stressful, if not overwhelming, at times. Sometimes, we need reminders to put work aside, to disconnect from social media and technology, and to focus on being with each other. In this section, there are several activities that help children develop self-care routines, and feel energized to continue moving toward their personal goals, family goals, and overall well-being. These tools will help them remember to take a moment to acknowledge their efforts and to recharge. Finally, this workbook concludes with self-care activities for the client and caregiver to allow the body and mind to refresh and strengthen its resiliency.

What Is Self-Care?

· ·

Self-care activities are simple moments that you take for yourself to unwind and recharge. Engaging in daily self-care is important for your body, mind, and emotions. How do you take care of yourself? Review the self-care examples provided here, and then brainstorm ways you can take care of your body, mind, and emotions.

- Quality time with friends/family

- Journaling

- Laughing

- Eating a healthy, balanced diet

- Getting enough sleep

- Exercising

- Mediating

- Reading

- Doing puzzles

Physical self-care: What are ways you can promote a healthy body?

Mental self-care: What are ways you can promote a healthy mind?

Emotional self-care: What are ways you can promote healthy emotions?

How Do You Self-Care?

. . . .

Self-care activities can either prepare us for a stressful situation or help us unwind once the situation is over. Some people prefer physical forms of self-care, like taking a walk or playing a sport, while others prefer mindfulness activities, like meditating or listening to music. Take this self-care survey and find out what activities you prefer. After a long day or times of stress, what helps you relax or recharge? The next challenge is to ask two friends or family members the same questions. What do you share with others, and what new activities could you try?

My favorite place to relax is:

Me: _____

Person #1: _____

Person #2: _____

My favorite comfort food is:

Me: _____

Person #1: _____

Person #2: _____

My favorite type of movement or exercise to relieve stress is:

Me: _____

Person #1: _____

Person #2: _____

My favorite sound to listen to when I am recharging (e.g., music, nature) is:

Me: _____

Person #1: _____

Person #2: _____

My favorite person to talk to after a hard day is:	How often do you practice self-care activities?
Me: _____	Me: _____
Person #1: _____	Person #1: _____
Person #2: _____	Person #2: _____

List three new ideas or activities that you can try when you need to recharge:

1. _____

2. _____

3. _____

Self-Care for the Senses

One way to practice self-care is to engage your five senses: hearing, taste, smell, vision, and touch. This worksheet provides some examples of self-care activities involving these senses, followed by some space for you to brainstorm your own ideas. Mark what activities you have tried and what you would like to try in the future to take care of your body and mind. Complete this exercise on your own or with a trusted person!

	Examples
Hearing	Listening to soothing music, hearing familiar voices, listening to audiobooks
Taste	Eating favorite foods, drinking water or tea, eating healthy food
Smell	Breathing in the fresh air, lighting scented candles, smelling essential oils
Vision	Watching a favorite TV show, reading, seeing family or friends
Touch	Wrapping up in a comfy blanket, sitting in a favorite chair, hugging a loved one

	My Example	Have Tried	Will Try
Hearing			
Taste			
Smell			
Vision			
Touch			

Client Worksheet

Self-Care Challenge

· ·

Brainstorm five different ways to nourish your mind and body and consider how you will make time for it. Then, take a self-care challenge! Commit to your self-care plan by challenging yourself to engage in these activities on a daily, weekly, and monthly basis.

Five ways to care for my mind:

1. _____

2. _____

3. _____

4. _____

5. _____

Five ways to care for my body:

1. _____

2. _____

3. _____

4. _____

5. _____

How will I take care of myself today?

I will take care of my mind by _____

I will take care of my body by _____

How will I take care of myself this week?

I will take care of my mind by _____

I will take care of my body by _____

How will I take care of myself this month?

I will take care of my mind by _____

I will take care of my body by _____

Checking In

Were you able to meet your self-care goals?   Yes   or   No

How can you make self-care part of your daily routine?

_____

_____

_____

_____

_____

Unplugging to Recharge

. . . .

Screen time is an easy way to disconnect, especially after a difficult day. But too much screen time can interfere with sleep, make it hard to burn off energy, and become an unhealthy habit. Take this challenge to unplug and unwind. Replace 15 minutes of screen time with a self-care activity of your choice, like playing a game, writing a letter, reading, or taking the dog for a walk. Write your ideas here and check off each day you are able to complete the challenge!

	New Activity	I did it!
Sunday		
Monday		
Tuesday		
Wednesday		
Thursday		
Friday		
Saturday		

How do you feel about replacing screen time with a self-care activity?

_____

_____

How can you make self-care part of your daily routine?

_____

_____

Mundane to Meaningful

. . . .

Day-to-day family activities are a great opportunity for interactions that allow for bonding, problem solving, and working together. Frequently, we don't take advantage of these opportunities because we see these activities as mundane chores, and we focus on completing them versus taking advantage of the journey. In this challenge, identify three activities that you do every week. Then, choose a single activity and consider which family members could participate and what role they could have in the activity. By assigning clear roles and responsibilities, everyone has a purpose and a reason to participate. Finally, reflect on the activity. How did everyone feel about their role?

Step 1: Identify three ordinary weekly activities:

• Grocery Shopping

• _____

• _____

Step 2: Choose an activity:

• _____

Step 3: Assign roles and responsibilities

Family Member	Role in Activity
Example: Caregiver	Example: Create a list for the store and find all the dairy items.

Step 4: Reflection
How was the activity? Would you want to do your role again?

_____

_____

_____

Thanking the Stars

. . . .

Gratitude helps us focus on the positive aspects of our life. Even if those aspects are small, they are important and help distract us from the negative influences around us. There are more positive aspects in your life than you realize. Complete this activity with your caregiver to identify what you are grateful for. First, work together to create a definition of what gratitude means to you. Then, take turns creating a thankful star recognizing something to be grateful for in your life. Be sure to include important relationships, events, memories, and successes.

What does it mean to be grateful?

Gratitude means...

_____

_____

What are you grateful for?

"Me Time" Schedule

. . . .

Track your self-care journey by writing down when and how you engaged in self-care this week. For example, maybe you exercised or talked to a close friend. Take note of how you felt before and after your self-care activity. By writing down these activities and looking at their impact, you can motivate yourself to make self-care part of your daily routine. Give yourself kudos for taking time for YOU!

	How did you feel before?	Self-care activity	How did you feel afterward?
Sunday			
Monday			
Tuesday			
Wednesday			
Thursday			
Friday			
Saturday			

You Are Loved

. . . .

Thank yourself for putting in the work to build your social-emotional abilities!

References

[1] Murphey, D., & Sacks, V. (2018). *The prevalence of adverse childhood experiences, nationally, by state, and by race or ethnicity.* Retrieved from https://www.childtrends.org/publications/prevalence-adverse-childhood-experiences-nationally-state-race-ethnicity

[2] Centers for Disease Control and Prevention. (2019). *About adverse childhood experiences.* Retrieved from https://www.cdc.gov/violenceprevention/childabuseandneglect/acestudy/aboutace.html

[3] Substance Abuse and Mental Health Services Administration. (n.d.). *Trauma, trauma types, and impact.* Retrieved from https://www.integration.samhsa.gov/clinical-practice/trauma-informed

[4] Centers for Disease Control and Prevention. (2019). *About adverse childhood experiences.* Retrieved from https://www.cdc.gov/violenceprevention/childabuseandneglect/acestudy/aboutace.html

[5] Center on the Developing Child, Harvard University. (n.d.). *Toxic stress.* Retrieved from https://developingchild.harvard.edu/science/key-concepts/toxic-stress/

[6] Bartlett, J., & Sacks, V. (2019, April 10). Adverse childhood experiences are different than child trauma, and it's critical to understand why. *Child Trends Blog.* Retrieved from https://www.childtrends.org/adverse-childhood-experiences-different-than-child-trauma-critical-to-understand-why

[7] Substance Abuse and Mental Health Services Administration. (2014). *SAMSHA's concept of trauma and guidance for a trauma-informed approach.* HHS Publication No. (SMA) 14-4884. Rockville, MD: Substance Abuse and Mental Health Services Administration.

Made in United States
North Haven, CT
08 September 2024

57192243R00104